Advanced Praise for
Trust Matters More than Ever

This is a must-read book for anyone seeking to elevate their leadership skills, deepen their relationships, and achieve lasting results. Trust MATTERS, and Horsager delivers the roadmap for building it.

—**Paul E. Funk II**, Four-Star General, U.S. Army (Ret.)

Thank you, David Horsager, for illustrating how a universal truth can be integrated in our daily work. The trust Rwandans have in their leadership has been the crucial engine that steered a nation reduced to ashes just 30 years ago towards peace and development. Renewed trust has allowed Rwandans to think, to plan, and to erect a more solid and better system than they have ever had before.

—**Ambassador Mathilde Mukantabana**
of the Republic of Rwanda to the USA

To trust or not to trust? My colleague and trusted friend, David Horsager, has the answer in this great and must-read book. He's right. It matters more than ever!

—**Mark Victor Hansen**, Founder and Co-creator of
Chicken Soup for the Soul book series

Navigating the intricate dynamics of trust in public service is paramount for a U.S. member of Congress to be successful. *Trust Matters More than Ever* doesn't just underscore its importance, it also provides tangible strategies, grounded in research and essential for fostering genuine connections with constituents and colleagues in today's political landscape.

—**Thomas W. Reed II**, Member of U.S. Congress
(NY, 2010-2022)

In *Trust Matters More than Ever*, David Horsager articulates why building trust across the aisle matters and what we can each do about it. His work is a testament to the power of trust in forging lasting, bipartisan partnerships. As someone who has always believed in working together for the common good, I find this book to be a vital resource for any leader seeking to unite rather than divide.

—**Max Rose**, Member of U.S. Congress (NY, 2019-2021)

David Horsager's latest work, *Trust Matters More than Ever*, is a timely masterpiece for leaders navigating the complexities of today's world.

—**Honorable Sam Poghisio**, Former Senate Majority Leader of Republic of Kenya

Every page of *Trust Matters More than Ever* is packed with tools and insights the reader can immediately apply in their work and personal life. Trust is the cornerstone for effective leadership in today's complex world. When it comes to helping leaders build trusted teams, no one does it better than David Horsager!

—**Lori Grant**, Associate Executive Director of Illinois Association of School Boards

David Horsager is the leading voice on the importance of being a trusted leader, inspiring organizations to cultivate leaders committed to building trust. He is the world's foremost authority on trust and his latest work contains powerful insights and practical tools to help leaders solve the most difficult challenges they face today.

—**Anthony Diekemper**, CEO of Rampart Communications

Trust Matters More than Ever offers a clear, comprehensive, and practical path forward for leaders in a world where trust is tanking. It's also a prescription for a life of integrity.

—**William J. Doherty**, Ph.D., Professor of Family Social Science, University of Minnesota, Co-founder of Braver Angels

Trust is harder to earn today than ever before. I am grateful that David Horsager has given us a playbook so we can build stronger, better, and more healthy relationships with those we seek to serve.

—**Donald Miller**, Author of *Building a StoryBrand*

David Horsager is a top-tier speaker, and he also transforms corporations. It's the stickiness of his research and the principles of his Trust Tools that will elevate your company and boost your bottom line. *Trust Matters More than Ever* is an easy and very practical resource for the busy leader.

—**Jerry Pattengale**, Ph.D., Author of *The World's Greatest Book, Inexplicable,* and *Public Intellectuals and the Common Good*

Without trust, transactions cannot occur, influence is diminished, and companies lose their best people. David Horsager's extensive research into what creates (or destroys) trust is something every leader needs to have in their back pocket. *Trust Matters More than Ever* is instantly implementable and will help you lead change, increase productivity, and improve your culture—it's working for us!

—**Jon S. Kulaga**, Ph.D., President of Indiana Wesleyan University

In law enforcement, there is little to no room for misconception. David Horsager's material swiftly propelled us into the future by motivating personal development, collaboration, unity, and kindness through simple yet profound content. I am infinitely grateful for the shared wisdom of how much TRUST MATTERS.

—**Michele Freeman**, Ph.D., Chief, City of Las Vegas Department of Public Safety (Ret.)

Trust Matters More than Ever knocks it out of the park! It gets to the heart of how trust is at the core of creating a winning culture in any organization.

—**Greg Feasel**, President of Colorado Rockies

As a former National Football League (NFL) player, coach, and chaplain, and a current NFL Players Association executive, I know firsthand how important trust is across the entire NFL organization. Horsager offers practical, actionable, evidence-based material for any business or leader who wants to win!

—**Dr. Don Davis**, Senior Director of Player Affairs of the National Football League Players Association

Polen Capital has worked with David Horsager to strengthen trust within our team. *Trust Matters More than Ever* has a practical focus with applicable tools that we can put to use right away.

—**Stan Moss**, CEO of Polen Capital

In a world that's craving authenticity and reliability, David Horsager's *Trust Matters More than Ever* is the go-to manual for leaders who aspire to cultivate a bedrock of trust in an era of skepticism. As expected, Horsager's work is research-based, brimming with actionable advice and Trust Tools that are as applicable to your personal life as they are to your career.

—**JJ Virgin**, 4x *New York Times* Bestselling Author, Celebrity Nutrition and Fitness Expert

Horsager hits the mark on what plagues the American small business and what we can all do to improve the environments we operate in. This is a roadmap for trust! Never before has it been more critical to utilize and deploy these 40 tools.

—**Brian Slipka**, Founder and CEO of True North Family of Companies

If building the most important asset you will ever own is important to you, read and fiercely apply the Trust Tools in this book!

—**Bobby Herrera**, President of Populus Group, Author of *The Gift of Struggle*

Trust Matters More than Ever, is jam-packed with fresh, succinct, research-based advice that will re-energize your organization and give you a solid foundation from which to lead.

—**"Famous Dave" Anderson**, America's Rib King,
National BBQ Hall of Fame

Trust and leadership go hand in hand. People of all levels of leadership will find *Trust Matters More than Ever* to be fresh and helpful!

—**Stephanie Chung**, Chief Growth Officer of Wheels UP,
First African American President in Aviation

With increasing political, cultural, economic, and social polarization in today's world, trust is ever shrinking. This book not only builds the case for trust, but it also lays out a framework for doing such. I have implemented these principles and tools in my own leadership journey across the land grant system in the United States. I have seen the impact of this critical work.

—**Brent D. Hales**, Ph.D., Associate Vice President,
Research and Cooperative Extension,
University of California Agriculture and Natural Resources

Trust Matters More than Ever is a must read for aspiring leaders. Horsager's brilliance is evident with fresh material underpinned by data. It's all about the "how" of building, maintaining, and restoring trust when it has been broken. His 8-Pillar approach to building trust is universal; it applies to the military, parenting, any business or industry, and even our own personal relationships!

—**John F. Meier**, Rear Admiral, U.S. Navy (Ret.)

DAVID HORSAGER

TRUST
MATTERS
MORE THAN EVER

*40 Proven Tools to Lead Better,
Grow Faster & Build Trust NOW!*

BroadStreet Publishing Group, LLC.
Savage, Minnesota, USA
Broadstreetpublishing.com

Trust Matters More than Ever
© 2024 David Horsager

A Horsager Leadership book.

9781424568918
9781424568925 eBook

Design services and Trust Tool art by Heidi Koopman, Purpose Design
Pillar art by Isaiah Horsager
Editing by Lisa Horsager, Heidi Sheard, and Michelle Winger

Printed in China.

24 25 26 27 28 29 30 7 6 5 4 3 2 1

*Dedicated to the trustworthy leaders
who consistently do what's right
over what's easy.*

Contents

Can I
trust
you?

Why Trust Matters

Trust is your greatest asset.

EVERY HUMAN IS HARDWIRED to measure trust. A newborn baby first looks for faces, eyes, and mouths. By six months, their brains have "a perception of trustworthiness" based on facial recognition.[1] This drive for connection does not disappear with age. These first impression judgments,[2] as social psychologists call them, become more sophisticated as we grow older, but the question remains the same.

Can I trust you?

In your daily interactions with others, you might think the question in everyone's mind is, *Do I like you?* but the more important question, and the question everyone is actually asking is, *Can I trust you?*

Can I trust this Uber driver to transport me safely?

Can I trust this financial advisor to give me sound advice?

Can I trust this doctor to help me?

Can I trust this company with my personal contact information?

Can I trust this teacher to educate my child well?

Trust is the fundamental backbone of relationships, society, performance, and growth. We follow leaders we trust. We buy, learn, drive, get married, put our kids on school buses, take prescription medicine, and put money in the bank all because we trust. The greatest asset you have in *every* relationship is trust.

Think about it. The only reason I put a lock on my bike, gate, or mailbox is because I don't trust people. The cost isn't just the price of the lock, it's the time it takes to open...close...open...close...open...close...

How long does it take to text message someone you trust? Boom, you are done in no time. How long does it take to message someone you don't trust? FOREVER! You worry about every word and wonder: *How will they perceive my message? How might they misconstrue it?* A lack of trust costs in every way.

If you don't trust the friends your teenager is hanging out with on Friday night, it's a huge emotional worry. If you don't trust a colleague on your team, it's your biggest cause of stress. What is your quality of life like when you don't trust your boss or your spouse?

Everything takes longer and costs more when trust is low.

Nothing affects the bottom line more than trust. According to Deloitte,[3] trusted companies outperform their market peers by up to 400%.

Our annual research publication, *Trust Outlook®*, has found:

- The majority of millennials say they would be more loyal to their employer, and they would put in longer hours, if they could trust their employer.

- The top reason people want to work for an organization is **trusted leadership**. It is rated higher than a raise, good benefits, more autonomy, or a fun work environment.

- More than 12 million Americans reported having invested $100,000 or more based purely on trusting someone else.

- When employees trust senior leadership, they offer more ideas and solutions, are better team players, and are significantly more loyal.

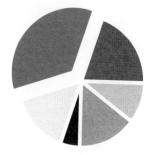

What's the #1 reason people want to work for an organization?
Trusted leadership!
Trust Outlook®

Defining Trust

Trust is a confident belief in someone or something. Trust itself is neutral; people can confidently believe in you for either positive or negative outcomes. If I am consistently late, you will begin to *trust* me to be late!

For the purpose of this book, we will define trust as:

**A confident belief in a person
to do what is good and right
on a consistent basis.**

Positive trust creates an enormous advantage and produces relationships that can significantly influence the people and the environment around them for the better. When you learn how to build trust—in yourself, your family, your team, your organization, and your community—you'll discover that everything else improves. Relationships, work performance, stress levels, confidence, physical health—*everything* starts with trust.

Organizations Don't Change.
People Change.

It could be tempting to think of someone else who "*really* needs to read this book on trust." While you might be right, the only person you can actually change is YOU. Ultimately, the most profound impact I've witnessed from this work has been personal. It changed my work life and my home life. It changed *me*.

Trust Is Complex

It's easy to think we know it all about trust, yet people seem to have different pictures of what trust is and how it works. To broaden our understanding of trust, below are a few nuances to consider:

- Trust must be given, and it must be earned.
- Trust can be supported by evidence, yet it can be a feeling in your gut.

- Trust can be built or broken in seconds, or it can take years to accumulate or erode.
- Trust is built through transparency and through confidentiality.
- Trust takes vulnerability and is always a risk.
- Trust requires investment and is one of the most critical forms of capital.
- There are good reasons not to trust someone or something.
- Trust can be used for good and for bad. (A mafia boss can be good at building trust.)

The Impact of Trust

Trust is the currency of business and life. When trust increases, morale, productivity, and revenue follow suit. When trust decreases, everything is more costly, stressful, and slow.

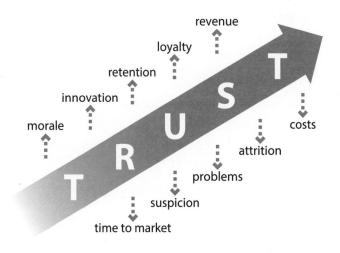

Without trust, everything from relationships and businesses to whole economies and governments are vulnerable to collapse. "When people lose trust in leadership," according to Gallup, "their decisions are informed by suspicion and their actions by self-interest. Businesses become more vulnerable as fewer employees are motivated to act for the greater good."[4]

I've seen this happen repeatedly. At best, skepticism and suspicion restrict the flow of ideas and reduce the ability to solve problems. At worst, they undermine the entire mission of your organization. An institution can have a great vision and capable employees, but it will still fail if its leadership is not trusted.

We can intuitively see how trust, or lack thereof, impacts our time, our finances, and our emotional health. In work, just like in our personal lives, we often blame things that are actually just symptoms of the core trust problem. Business problems are never really about leadership, communication, sales, engagement, marketing, or finances. At the core, the solutions are always established through trust.

> "
> *When the Captain and I implemented the TELI material with our leadership team, we improved trust among the crew, which increased their ability to come to their leaders about sensitive mental health issues.*
> —**Lawrence Comdeco, Jr.**, U.S. Navy Command Master Chief (Ret.)
> "

Problems exist—and persist— because of a lack of trust.

A Breach of Trust Can Destroy

International tensions. Business failures. Family divisions. Economic collapses. Political discord. Low trust magnifies broken relationships and systems and costs society an exorbitant amount of money.

- According to FDIC, the failure of Silicon Valley Bank and Signature Bank in 2023 cost $22 billion.[5]

- The Catholic Church paid nearly $4 billion to victims of abuse in the past decade.[6]

- "Deflategate," the National Football League scandal alleging that the New England Patriots deflated (or knowingly used) deflated footballs during the 2014 AFC title game cost $22.5 million.[7]

- Volkswagen says their 2015 diesel emissions scandal cost them $34.7 billion.[8]

Saying, "Just trust me" isn't trusted. Trust is earned.

Paul J. Zak, director of the Center for Neuroeconomics Studies, conducted research on levels of oxytocin and stress hormones and how they affected a person's performance. Zak discovered, unsurprisingly, that stress is a strong inhibitor to trust.

Conversely, when trust levels at an organization are high, people report:

- 74% less stress
- 50% higher productivity
- 76% more engagement
- 40% less burnout.[9]

Trust Is a Leading Indicator of Success

We frequently look for leading and lagging indicators in business. In our global work, we have seen trust is always a leading indicator of success. Trust levels end up being a *very* accurate, predictive measure of either failure or success! That's why it's critical to actively prevent gaps in trust and close any breaches that already exist.

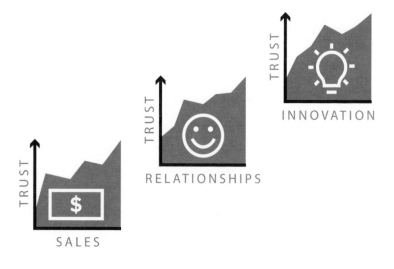

SALES

RELATIONSHIPS

INNOVATION

Trust is *always* the CORE issue!

Your Single Most Valuable Asset

Scan any company's balance sheet and you'll find a measure of trust behind every number. It's not something typically thought of as having an economic value, but when you scratch the surface of all those numbers, you will find that where trust is lower, the reported numbers are too.

For instance, with greater trust, customers will pay premiums, freely promote your business, and return again and again. With suppliers we trust, delivery time and costs decrease because there is less need for double-checking, paperwork, and follow-up. When trust fuels your processes, every aspect of your organization becomes more streamlined and more profitable.

Trust Works

What happens when leaders and organizations make trust-building a strategic priority? At Trust Edge Leadership Institute (TELI), we have had the opportunity to witness the transformation of people and organizations firsthand. When people prioritize solving with trust, the results speak for themselves!

- A $1 billion global dealership group increased their market share 11% in one year.

- A multibillion-dollar insurance company increased their engagement score for the first time in 14 years.

- A mid-sized healthcare company eliminated $2.4 million in attrition costs in nine months.

- A college football team's record went from 3–7 one year to 7–3 the very next year.

- A salesperson tripled sales in 90 days.

Personal trust is back.

TRUST MATTERS

CLARITY

COMPASSION

CHARACTER

COMPETENCY

COMMITMENT

CONNECTION

CONTRIBUTION

CONSISTENCY

SOLVE WITH TRUST

What Happened to Trust?

A full-circle story.

A LONG, LONG TIME AGO, trust was personal, and it depended on proximity. There were two basic reasons people didn't trust others:

Reason 1: "I *don't* know you. You're unfamiliar to me, so I don't trust you."

Reason 2: "I *do* know you. I've seen how you act; therefore, I don't trust you."

As populations increased and communities expanded, governments, schools, businesses, and economic systems were formed to support new societal structures. People began to trust whole institutions rather than relying on individual relationships. We moved from *personal* trust to *institutional* trust.

Institutional trust is the foundation of our laws, contracts, and entire economic system, and has the benefit of being upheld even when there is an occasional breach of personal trust. We could have a bad teacher without losing trust in the entire education system. We could suffer one bad politician and not lose confidence in the government to act in our country's overall best interests.

Institutional trust in America was quite strong in the early 1960s with around 77% of Americans believing the government would do what is right. Now, only two Americans out of 10 say they would trust the federal government to do what is right.[10]

Do you trust the government to do what is right?

Pew Research, "Public Trust in Government: 1958-2023"

Low Institutional Trust

The effects of distrust and low trust are readily seen across institutions from government, education, and religion to media, healthcare, and food.

- *We are losing confidence in our education system.* When I was young, homeschooling was uncommon. Now it is one of the fastest growing forms of education in the United States.[11]

- **We are losing faith in religion.** Even though roughly the same number of people say they believe in God as did decades ago, both attendance and financial giving at places of worship are down significantly.[12]

- **We don't trust our news.** Trust in mainstream media is even lower than government! Many can remember a time when we had "the news." Now, one person has her news, and another person has his news. Our growing distrust in the media is having profound effects on our society.

- **We no longer blindly accept the "doctor's orders."** The institution of modern medicine has seen a decline in trust due to increased public access to expert information, healthcare complexity, patient empowerment, and historical injustices.[13]

In recent years, we've moved from institutional trust to *distributed* trust. Distributed trust means multiple independent sources combine to give the consumer confidence. Airbnb, Uber, and blockchain technology are all examples of distributed trust. Have you ever felt better about purchasing a product or eating at a restaurant because of a rating system? Institutional trust and distributed trust clearly play an important role in our society, but we are seeing signs that there is an increasing preference for direct communication and face-to-face interactions. People want to *know* the person before they decide whether or not to extend trust.[14] It's the reason trust in small businesses is at an all-time high. Personal trust is back.

> The more personal we can be,
> the more trusted we will be.

More
than ever.

CLARITY

COMPASSION

CHARACTER

COMPETENCY

COMMITMENT

CONNECTION

CONTRIBUTION

CONSISTENCY

SOLVE WITH TRUST

Trust Matters NOW

Trust is timeless and timely.

WHILE TRUST HAS ALWAYS BEEN both timely and timeless, a growing body of research suggests that modern life—in all of its high-tech, high-speed, high-resolution glory—is creating a situation where trust has never been more valuable or more breakable. Below are ten reasons why the critical factor of trust is on the rise and why it matters NOW more than ever.

1. *Human connection is vanishing.* Remote workers, social media, and artificial intelligence (AI) are taking us further and further from the reality of in-person connections and bringing us to conveniently designed digital experiences. People today can even have AI girlfriends and boyfriends, so they don't have to deal with the work of a real partner.

2. *Isolation is increasing.* Despite our ability to "connect" to more people than ever before, we are the loneliest

we've ever been. A recent Gallup study reports that one in four people throughout the world feel "lonely" on a regular basis.[15] According to Dr. Vivek H. Murthy, Surgeon General of the United States of America, "Loneliness is far more than just a bad feeling—it harms both individual and societal health. It is associated with a greater risk of cardiovascular disease, dementia, stroke, depression, anxiety, and...loneliness increases the risk of premature death as much as smoking fifteen cigarettes per day."[16]

> ## Trust is the cornerstone of connection and community, and we need it more than ever.

3. *We are losing our grip on reality.* The line between what is real and what isn't real has blurred more than ever. *What does that person actually look like? Is it #nofilter or #reallife? Is this a deepfake or an authentic image? What numbers are truly reliable?* When we spend more time scrolling through 30-second videos than we do having conversations with friends, it is no surprise that our ability to discern reality becomes distorted. Dissociation, derealization, and depersonalization are just a few examples of disorders tied to losing a sense of what is real. "These conditions include escape from reality in ways that are not wanted and not healthy. This causes problems in managing everyday life."[17]

4. *We are more interdependent than ever.* Thanks to advancements in technology and transportation, more and more people are crossing time zones, borders, and oceans with ease—often

with a click of a button. It's easy to take for granted the amount of interconnectedness necessary for a normal day to unfold. A single data breach in a financial institution can instantly affect millions of people all over the planet. One cyberattack on the power grid or one moral failure of a major leader can have implications that are fast, harsh, and far-reaching.

5. ***Political division is incentivized.*** A hundred years ago in the United States, Democrat and Republican members of Congress would debate vehemently on the floor, then ride the train back to their home state, amicably eating and drinking together as friends. In my recent work on Capitol Hill, I learned that after freshman orientation, new members of congress are whisked away in different vehicles and stay at separate hotels based on their political party. Congressional leaders might even be stripped of responsibilities such as committee assignments if they try to work across the aisle.

6. ***Self-centered thinking is celebrated.*** Instant gratification, a lack of personal responsibility, rising litigation, and poor customer service are all indicators that selfishness has chipped away at societal trust. Social media influencers are praised when they act arrogantly and divisively. The community virtues of selflessness, honor, and serving the common good are seldom encouraged, and in fact are diminished via hyped-up, personal branding and ego-boosting tactics. Despite this trend, a team's success greatly depends on whether the individuals are in it together or in it for themselves.

7. ***Unknowns create fear.*** Increased global crisis awareness and biased information has created an environment of uncertainty. Unknowns produce fear, and fear jeopardizes trust.

8. ***Technology holds our private information.*** Digitization makes it convenient to save and share private information, but it can also make us vulnerable. We sometimes don't even know where or how our information is shared, nor do we know what the security repercussions could be. From booking rentals to buying tickets to conducting bank transfers, new technology has changed how we live.

9. ***Negativity produces more negativity.*** Negative news and social media stories magnify the worst of humanity. When we are exposed repeatedly to emotions like anger, fear, disgust, and confusion, they start to feel normal. A recent survey of people who say they prefer to watch news coverage that is political in nature revealed that 82% of the news coverage they watch is mostly negative![18] Basic psychology teaches us that we tend to get more of what we focus on. A culture that normalizes distrust will deteriorate.

10. ***Society has become trust conscious.*** People aren't just appreciating the value of trust; they are starving for it. When I started my research on trust, there was very little published on the topic. I used to have to prove the bottom-line impact of trust. Now, forward-thinking organizations see the competitive advantage and readily invest in building cultures of trust.

Trust is grown or diminished in every interaction, whether you know it or not.

Your Biggest Risk

Trust really does matter now more than ever. In fact, losing trust is your biggest risk. Trust can take a long time to build, yet it can be wiped out in a moment. Without doing the active, conscious work that is required to build trust, there is a natural drift away from it. Rebuilding trust is costly, and it does not automatically flow from good intentions.

> **"**
> *Our trust work has revolutionized our approach and led to a pivotal change in turnover rates, reducing them from 40% to 10%.*
> —**David Cameron**, City Administrator of City of Republic
> **"**

One of the most rewarding insights we've gained about trust is not only how pivotal it is, but also how *available* it is. Trust is a core competency that you *can* build, rebuild, strengthen, measure, and use for the benefit of you and everyone around you. At TELI, we've heard everything from, "We increased engagement scores by double digits," and "It saved us millions of dollars," to "It restored my marriage."

Solve Real Problems with Trust

In the following pages, you'll find a proven framework and 40 Trust Tools, including ones that will teach you how to:

- get the most important goal done every day,
- create accountability that works,
- communicate clear expectations,
- motivate your team to get results,
- increase trust during conflict,
- ...and more!

CLARITY | COMPASSION | CHARACTER | COMPETENCY | COMMITMENT | CONNECTION | CONTRIBUTION | CONSISTENCY | SOLVE WITH TRUST

It has never been more important to talk about trust, and there has never been a better time to build it. Everywhere I go people say, "We need more trust here." If you want to become a more trustworthy leader who influences your company and the world for good—if you want to make a difference—then the most important leadership work you've ever done starts NOW.

The greatest businesses of our time are *differentiating* with TRUST.

8 Pillars of Trust

The Framework

A Firm Foundation.

THROUGH A COMBINATION of my original graduate work, our decades of research at TELI, and my experience helping people and organizations, I've uncovered *eight specific traits* that the most trusted leaders, brands, and organizations have in common. These eight traits form a framework for how trust is built.

Like the columns of a building, these pillars hold up the whole entity of trust. When one or more of the pillars is weakened or cracked, stress is put on the other pillars, and the entire structure is in danger of collapsing.

Let's dig into the 8 Pillars of Trust.

The 8 Pillars have plenty of support from the scientific literature and from the empirical data we collected. It's a model for how these kinds of frameworks should be built.

—**Josh Packard**, Ph.D, Executive Director, Social Research Lab, University of Northern Colorado

TRUST MATTERS

CLARITY

COMPASSION

CHARACTER

COMPETENCY

COMMITMENT

CONNECTION

CONTRIBUTION

CONSISTENCY

SOLVE WITH TRUST

The 8 Pillars of Trust

Pillar 1: Clarity

People trust what is clear and simple. They distrust what is ambiguous or overly complex. A leader might not be trusted if they are not clear about the vision. A manager will not be trusted if they are not clear about expectations. A salesperson might be clear about how knowledgeable they are, but until they get clear about the benefits of the product, no one buys.

Pillar 2: Compassion

People put faith in those who care beyond themselves. If you don't have care or positive intent beyond yourself, people will have a hard time following you or being accountable to you. Compassion builds trust; hatefulness and apathy destroy it.

Increased understanding of the 8-Pillar Framework coupled with team and self-assessments has activated school leaders on their journey of personal and professional growth. They are experiencing deeper relationships with their teams and those they serve.

—**Cindy Swenson**, District Strategy Partner, Sourcewell

Pillar 3: Character

People count on those who do what is right over what is easy. Those who are honest and selfless are trusted.

Pillar 4: Competency

People have confidence in those who stay fresh, relevant, and capable. If you are teaching, selling, or leading the same way you were 10 years ago, you might be losing trust. People trust those who keep learning and showing they are capable.

Pillar 5: Commitment

People believe in those who stand through adversity. If people think you might quit when the going gets tough, they won't follow you. They want to know you are going to stick with it and stick with them.

Pillar 6: Connection

People want to follow, buy from, and be around those who are willing to connect and collaborate. Silos and ego often kill this pillar. Solving big problems usually takes a deeper level of trust with a network of people. We need each other.

Pillar 7: Contribution

At the end of the day, people need to contribute results to be trusted. You might be good at the other pillars, like Compassion or Competency, but if you don't get the desired outcomes, trust will be lost.

Pillar 8: Consistency

People are wired to identify patterns and predictable behaviors. Reputations and brands are only as strong as they are consistent. People want to know you are going to show up and deliver the same way every time in spite of the circumstances.

> The 8 Pillars of Trust are
> the foundation of a
> high-performance life.

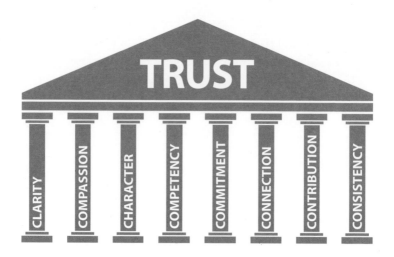

The Pillars Work Together

I have used the 8 Pillars of Trust to help build (or rebuild) trust in global governments, professional sports teams, big and small corporations, and nonprofit companies. While it is always vital to consider the context of your culture or situation, you can be confident that any problem, in any sphere, will fall under one or more of the pillars.

People might believe they have a leadership, sales, or communication issue. But at the core, it is a result of a weakened pillar. For example, clear communication is trusted while ambiguous or complex communication is not (Clarity Pillar). Compassionate communication is trusted, hateful communication is not (Compassion Pillar). Wise counsel is trusted; incompetent advice is not (Competency Pillar). Using the pillars, you can solve the *real* communication issue. The good news is that you can identify and solve your core issues when you drill down and use the 8 Pillars of Trust.

The elements in the 8-Pillar Framework are relatively coequal and work together to build and reinforce trust. For example, you might have clarity for a moment by sharing the vision at the annual meeting, but if you don't share that message *consistently,* then you lose it. For the foundation of trust to stand, all pillars need to be present, healthy, and strong!

However, in a given situation, some of these eight traits may be more important than others. If you are hiring a nanny for your children, you may prioritize Compassion and Character over Clarity. If a surgeon is going to operate on you, you may not be too concerned with Connection, but you will be keenly interested in Competency!

Why Trust Tools?

While I care deeply about being research-based, I've learned something; the research behind it doesn't matter if it's not actionable! The 40 Trust Tools in this book are simple, clear, and usable. They were crafted to make it easier to build the Pillars of Trust in your work and in your life.

Just like there are many tools for different tasks, there are many tools you can use to build trust. But you can't use all of them at once. Pick a single Trust Tool and try it. Once you have practiced it, pick up another tool and give it a try. One at a time, you'll learn which ones help the most in your current situation. You'll likely develop some favorites, and you'll have others you want to come back and try later.

This book is meant to serve as a resource for the various human issues and team challenges you need to solve. The next eight chapters start with stories and a discussion of why that specific pillar matters. At the end of each chapter, you'll find the most valuable methods, processes, and tools we've used in over two decades of developing high-trust cultures. Use the bookmark, write in the margins, and dog ear the pages. I hope this book will help you become both empowered and encouraged.

If you are acquainted with my work on trust, a few of the upcoming Trust Tools will look familiar. You'll see that they have evolved into a more complete resource and *many* more have been added. This is my most robust collection of Trust Tools.

It's time to put the pillars to work!

Specificity matters.

Pillar 1: Clarity

*People trust what is clear and
distrust what is ambiguous or overly complex.*

UNLESS YOUR COMPANY has a billion-dollar marketing budget, a simple, clear business name beats a cute, creative one. Consider Barb as a hypothetical example. She specializes in cutting hair and wants her customers to know her salon is a relaxing place to visit. She names her business *Whispers on Main*. The only problem is that no one driving by has any idea what kind of store it is. She changes her shop name to *Best Haircuts by Barb* and sees a huge increase in business.

In this noisy, busy, complicated world, ambiguity loses and clarity wins. Many people think they are communicating clearly, when in fact, they are not. Clarity of vision inspires. Clarity of expectations motivates. Clarity of directions gives confidence. Clarity of values aligns decision-making. Clarity of the assignment avoids frustrations. Clarity unifies. *Clarity wins.*

Why Does Clarity Matter?

- *Specificity always improves productivity.* Specific instructions improve the chances of the best outcome in training, at home, and in the board room.

- *Clarity reduces ambiguity and leads to better decisions.* Georgetown University found, "Information quality affects decision quality."[19] Where there is vagueness, poor decisions are likely.

- *You get what you ask for.* If you are not clear on what you want, you will never get it. Clear communication gets clear results.

- *A lack of clarity is costly.* We suffer from information and choice overload, and our businesses suffer financially when we don't get to the point.

- *Clarity reduces conflict.* Half of workplace conflict is due to a lack of clear communication.[20] If the message is clear, there is less room for misunderstanding. Unclear strategy and priorities cause misalignment.

Clarity Takes Work

Clarity unifies, aligns, and gives hope. It is unique among the pillars as the *quickest* path to building trust. Increase clarity and you'll swiftly see results. That being said, clarity also needs the *most maintenance*. It's like a sandcastle continually at risk of being washed away by waves. Noise gets in the way. Time goes by. People forget. It takes intentionality to maintain clarity on a team or in an organization.

Two Types of Clarity

1. Communication Clarity

The definition of communication is "shared meaning." We communicate every day with everyone we meet, and yet we never have perfect shared meaning because our interpretations are shaped by our different backgrounds, experiences, perspectives, and biases. Communication clarity includes everything from how we communicate expectations to how we deal with conflict.

2. Strategic Clarity

If your organization or team's strategy is not defined, it will be very difficult to communicate and follow. For an organization, strategic clarity ranges all the way from clarity on the mission to the priorities and daily goals.

A Delicate Balance

Communicating clearly is a nuanced balancing act! *Too little* information creates anxiety and uncertainty. *Too much* information creates anxiety and uncertainty.

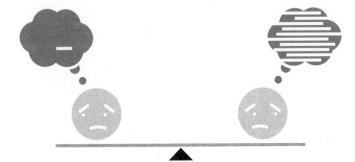

TRUST MATTERS

CLARITY

COMPASSION

CHARACTER

COMPETENCY

COMMITMENT

CONNECTION

CONTRIBUTION

CONSISTENCY

SOLVE WITH TRUST

Whether it's an airplane full of passengers or a company with thousands of employees in multiple locations, keeping people in the dark, even if it's bad news, can kill trust. On the other hand, sharing too many details is not wise either because complex or unnecessary information can bog down teams or promote rumors and the mishandling of information. Not everything in life or in business can or should be shared openly. Be as transparent as you *can* be, while being as confidential as you *ought* to be. It's a delicate but critical balance.

Clarity Gaps

What can you do if you find a clarity gap? Take responsibility for the miscommunication and quickly (and publicly) communicate the actions you are implementing in order to close it. Clarity breeds clarity, so the more you work toward adding it in any one area, the more it will positively affect and be replicated in other areas.

Conflict and interpersonal issues are examples of problems created by clarity gaps. Leadership expert Tony Gambill noted: "Workplace conflict is often interpreted as an interpersonal issue, but the root cause is usually because of misaligned or unclear goals and roles."[21] Clarity gaps take management time and can be a roadblock to achieving company alignment. Take time to get to the bottom of misalignment. Examine role expectations and realities. Clarify priorities.

> Clarity increases unity, cuts conflict, and accelerates results.

Clarity strengthens the other Pillars of Trust. For example:

- When we get clear on values, the Character Pillar will strengthen.

- When we are clear on the vision, the Connection Pillar will increase.

- When priorities and expectations are clear, the Commitment Pillar is empowered.

Don't underestimate the power of a little clarity.

Clarity in Action

Here are a few helpful examples of leaders investing in clarity:

- The president of a college initiated a new alignment practice by sending weekly "Memos from the President."

- A CEO started hosting a virtual "Ask me anything" time each month.

- The dean of a large university sent a video explaining the WHY concerning every new initiative being rolled out or cut.

- A high school teacher set a new process for clarity on assignments that students could understand and follow.

- A CTO started sharing the top three priorities of the company every week and asked all departments and employees to make sure their priorities aligned with them.

- A healthcare CEO used the How? How? How? Trust Tool you will soon learn to turn around a toxic culture.

- A salesperson dramatically increased sales when he got clear about the benefits of the product instead of just how great the company was.

- A school superintendent used the Survey Implementation Plan to complete all the goals on the district's strategic plan for the first time ever.

- A general manager began visiting every site once quarterly and shared the company's vision for 10 minutes.

- A Fortune 500 CEO started hearing the echo of the company's top priorities once he started sharing them clearly and consistently.

CLARITY TRUST TOOLS

Communication Clarity

#1 MRA Messages

#2 Two Qs for Relevancy

#3 ODC in Communication

#4 Four Ps of Meetings

#5 Survey Implementation Plan

Strategic Clarity

#6 MVP

#7 Priority Alignment

#8 How, How, How?

#9 90-Day Quick Plan

TRUST MATTERS
CLARITY
COMPASSION
CHARACTER
COMPETENCY
COMMITMENT
CONNECTION
CONTRIBUTION
CONSISTENCY
SOLVE WITH TRUST

Trust Tool #1: MRA MESSAGES™

Memorable. Repeatable. Actionable. You may believe whole-heartedly in the value of the message you are trying to convey. Unfortunately, it doesn't matter if people can't remember it.

MEMORABLE   **R**EPEATABLE   **A**CTIONABLE

Clarity determines value. For your message or brand to become trusted, it needs to be clear and simple. Memorize these three words by which to clarify any message whether a new marketing campaign or a chore list for your kids.

For values to be applied, they need to be memorable, repeatable, and actionable. For decision-making frameworks to be remembered and used, they need to be memorable, repeatable, and actionable.

The next time you are implementing a new plan or communicating a crucial message, run it through the MRA filter:

- ☐ Is it Memorable?
- ☐ Is it Repeatable?
- ☐ Is it Actionable?

MRA in Action

One of my favorite examples of *Memorable, Repeatable, Actionable* comes from Caribou Coffee's B.A.M.A. training for frontline employees in the 2000s. While they were growing to become the second-largest coffee chain in North America, I sat down with then CEO, Mike Tattersfield. He attributed much of the brand expansion, consistent experience, and high retention rates to a condensed barista training they called B.A.M.A.

B = Be Excellent not Average

A = Act with Urgency

M = Make a Connection

A = Anticipate Needs

People felt welcomed, received the same great mocha day in and day out, and often had their drink in hand before paying. The company's simple B.A.M.A. employee training model laid the groundwork for clarity that led to consistency, trust, and success in the years when Caribou Coffee grew the fastest.

Caribou is experiencing another period of unprecedented growth around the globe, and the current CEO, John Butcher, is very good at honoring the best of the past while setting a relevant vision for what is ahead. He continues the tradition

TRUST MATTERS

CLARITY

COMPASSION

CHARACTER

COMPETENCY

COMMITMENT

CONNECTION

CONTRIBUTION

CONSISTENCY

SOLVE WITH TRUST

of crystal-clear messaging and recently talked me through the new purpose of Caribou Coffee: "To create day-making experiences that spark a chain reaction of good." You can see that, like the values of B.A.M.A., their purpose is *memorable, repeatable*, and *actionable*, whether you are a barista helping a wheelchair-bound customer or a general manager making hiring decisions. Clarity, not just quality coffee, has been a massive part of Caribou's success.

TRUST MATTERS

CLARITY

COMPASSION

CHARACTER

COMPETENCY

COMMITMENT

CONNECTION

CONTRIBUTION

CONSISTENCY

SOLVE WITH TRUST

> *Use this tool to make sure what you're saying*
> *matters to your audience.* –DH

Trust Tool #2:
TWO Qs FOR RELEVANCY™

I worked with an outstanding speech coach in the early years of my career. She taught me that every time you say anything at all, you must run your words through a mental filter of *What does it mean* **to the audience**? and *What does it mean* **right now**? Answering these questions forces clarity and improves connection with recipients.

COMPANY?
CUSTOMERS?

RIGHT
NOW?

The Two Questions

Explore these two key questions to ensure relevance of any message but especially when implementing change:

1. **What does it mean to our company or customers?**
   - How will our employees be affected by this change?
   - Who will be impacted the most?
   - If we put our feet in the shoes of our customers, how will this sound?

2. **What does it mean right now?**
   - What does this product launch mean for us amidst what's already happening?
   - What does this restructure mean to our team right now?
   - What does this change mean for us this year?

When you answer these questions, you stay relevant and trusted. It's important to have a shared understanding of the answers to these questions with your team members, so they are better able to internalize the message and act on its behalf.

A work example: "Hey everyone, we've uncovered a huge market for a new product. What this means for the company is that we are going to shift 30% of our resources and focus to this opportunity for the next 90 days. Each department will carry different portions of this weight. What it means for you on this team, for the remainder of the quarter, is that you will need to pause our international product line and redirect development dollars to the new market."

A personal example: "Hey kids, we have friends coming to stay with us this weekend. What this means for you is that we need help picking up the house and making some extra food. You need to get your homework done early and be ready to help for a couple of hours on Thursday right after school."

Maintain Your Relevance

"What does it mean to the group" and "what does it mean right now" can also be explored regularly to ensure that you are *staying* relevant with a mission or vision:

- What does our mission *mean* to our employees *today*?

- Is our vision *still coming across* the way we want it to?

- How are our customers experiencing us *this quarter*?

When you answer the relevancy questions, your internal team as well as your external partners and clients feel included and are more willing to listen. Ask these questions to make sure your message sticks.

Trust Tool #3: ODC IN COMMUNICATION™

My first leadership job was far from home, and I was leading people more experienced than myself. It taught me a lot, not the least of which was that the problem was often ME! I started using this Trust Tool with that team and mitigated my own tendency to be unclear.

OUTCOME   **D**EADLINE   **C**LARIFIERS

Clear communication is vital to productivity and workflow. The Outcome, Deadline, Clarifiers (ODC) helps managers give clear expectations so their people can win. Use these three important elements to fine-tune clarity when working toward your next big goal!

O – Outcome

Outcome is the goal explicitly explained. In the Outcome phase, you clearly communicate the vision or the desired end result of the project or goal. Take the time to think through what the outcome will look like for all stakeholders. The clearer the picture you can paint of the Outcome, the better chance everyone, including yourself, has of reaching the target.

D – Deadline

In the Deadline phase, you get extremely specific. Many leaders avoid giving an absolute deadline because they either assume it's under-

Numerous times, I have been surprised when a project I assigned to a team member does not even come close to hitting the mark. ODC has helped translate what is in my head to staff, resulting in less frustration all around!

—**Kassidy Rice**, Senior Director of Education Solutions, Sourcewell

stood, they don't realize they need one, or they are afraid it will create conflict. Here's what I've seen: Not giving a deadline usually creates conflict. If I say, "Let me know where we are at on this project soon," *soon* has different meanings to different people. A more effective statement would be, "Can I see the first draft at our 10 a.m. meeting?" When people are given a specific time, they are empowered to succeed.

C – Clarifiers

Ask questions to ensure clarity. This doesn't mean asking, "Are we clear?" as you rush out the door. Avoid yes or no answers and be kind. Word your questions in such a way that you show you expect there will be a need for clarification.

TRUST MATTERS

CLARITY

COMPASSION

CHARACTER

COMPETENCY

COMMITMENT

CONNECTION

CONTRIBUTION

CONSISTENCY

SOLVE WITH TRUST

For example:

- Does this plan need any tweaks?

- What questions come to mind when you visualize this in action?

- Are we missing any steps or potential barriers on the way to this outcome?

Both the requester and the clarifier need to drill down for understanding, repeating what they hear to make sure they are aligned on the priorities, expectations, and next steps.

ODC in Practice

One of our TELI employees got so good at this tool, it sped up every meeting she participated in! She was always quick to ask clarifying questions and never left without making sure there was a defined deadline. This benefited the whole team's productivity and left little margin for uncertainty or wasted effort.

> **"**
>
> *On a routine survey, we found that our crew had high trust (over 95%) in Command Leadership, but only 82% trust in their immediate department or divisional leadership. Most would be happy with a "B" grade, but the Captain and I knew it was something we wanted to get after. We implemented ODC and increased Mentoring. When we conducted another survey, trust in immediate leadership increased to 93%!*
>
> —**Lawrence Comdeco, Jr.**, U.S. Navy Command Master Chief (Ret.)
>
> **"**

ODC can work with your children too. When our kids were younger, we defined a "clean room" by just two things: 1) no clothes on the floor and 2) bedspread pulled over the pillow. We didn't focus on what toys were under the bed or what it looked like in the closet.

- *The Outcome:* "There should be no clothes on the floor and bedspread over the pillow."

- *The Deadline:* "It must be done before school and on non-school days before you can play with friends or 10 a.m., whichever comes first."

- *Clarifiers:* "Are we on the same page? Do you know where to put your clothes? Do you understand what it looks like to have both corners of the bedspread up over your pillow?"

I can't say it worked perfectly, but the clarity definitely helped eliminate arguments and gave our kids a chance at being successful.

Leaders of all kinds have the opportunity to practice the ODC in Communication Trust Tool. Are you good at one aspect of this method already and just need to improve the others? Here is your checklist. Try it tomorrow!

☐ Define the desired **Outcome**.

☐ Set and communicate the **Deadline**.

☐ Chase down the **Clarifiers** to achieve ultimate clarity for everyone.

TRUST MATTERS

CLARITY

COMPASSION

CHARACTER

COMPETENCY

COMMITMENT

CONNECTION

CONTRIBUTION

CONSISTENCY

SOLVE WITH TRUST

Trust Tool #4: FOUR Ps OF MEETINGS™

Meetings often get a bad rap because too many of them end up being unproductive and a waste of time. However, meetings *can* be the best way to communicate, collaborate, and accomplish important work. When should we choose to hold a meeting? Can we let go of some of them? How can we be more efficient? The Four Ps of Meetings include a predetermined *purpose*, the right *people*, a clear *plan*, and an effective *place*.

Make Meetings Matter

Don't schedule meetings unless you can satisfactorily provide each of the Four Ps.

P1 – A Clear Purpose

What's the purpose of this meeting? The more specific the better. What outcomes are you hoping for? Asking this question of yourself as the leader can help you realize you can combine one meeting with another, or perhaps you don't even need a meeting because the participants can effectively communicate another way. Communicate the purpose of the meeting before people arrive so they can help by being prepared. Always create unity and alignment by stating the purpose at the beginning of every meeting. No established purpose? No meeting needed.

> The Four Ps helped our meetings become 5x more productive.
> —**Daniel Kerrigan**, Chief of Staff, TELI

P2 – The Right People

Who should be at this meeting? Only those expected to contribute should be required. Stop inviting everyone to every meeting. Yes, be inclusive but not in a way that makes people unproductive. Sometimes it can be just as effective to have a peripheral team member weigh in with a message of input to the group before the meeting, allowing time for thought and discussion.

P3 – A Predetermined Plan

What's the plan for this meeting? Whether it's a goal or an agenda, have a basic plan for how the purpose of the meeting is going to be accomplished. The agenda should outline approximate times for doing the most important activities that will accomplish the purpose. If it is hard to come up with a plan, perhaps you just need a one-on-one meeting to take the next step.

P4 – An Effective Place

How could your choice of location impact your purpose for the meeting? Stand-up meetings, virtual meetings, and lunch meetings all provide different advantages. I like walking meetings when I debrief with one of my senior leaders. If your goal is primarily connection, you will want to avoid meeting in the same space where painful reviews or potential stress has repeatedly occurred. If the purpose is already intense or needs a lighthearted touch, perhaps a coffee shop feels more neutral or lowers the pressure. On the flip side, if your meeting is very important, it might be effective to meet in a more formal place.

Sometimes a small change can go a long way. To align the right place with your meeting's purpose, consider:

- How long will the meeting be?
- How private should the meeting be?
- How intense will the meeting be?

TRUST MATTERS

CLARITY

COMPASSION

CHARACTER

COMPETENCY

COMMITMENT

CONNECTION

CONTRIBUTION

CONSISTENCY

SOLVE WITH TRUST

> *The success of rolling out surveys goes up dramatically*
> *when leaders use this process.* ⎯DN

Trust Tool #5:
SURVEY IMPLEMENTATION PLAN™

Have you ever participated in an engagement survey and
wondered if the feedback was even implemented? Or have you
ever sent out a survey and been too busy to analyze, share, or
act on the results? Either of these scenarios can significantly
impact trust in an organization.

Use the Power of Surveys

We understand survey results are often overwhelming. I can't tell you how many times I've seen valuable information sit on a shelf. As we guide leaders through our Enterprise Trust Index™ results, we have a method that keeps leaders on task and motivated to make good use of the data. (Visit MeasureMyTrust.com for more.)

Following is our plan for release and roll out of survey information. Perhaps it will help you too.

1. **Share the overall findings quickly.**
   Whether through a townhall or all-team meeting, let your people know the basic findings as soon as you can after you receive the results. Include gratitude for their participation, a review of the important reasons you did the survey, a few highlight takeaways you plan to process, and your commitment to swift action. They need to feel it was worth their time to fill out the survey.

2. **Identify primary focus points.**
   You won't be able to act on every recommendation revealed in a survey right away and people understand that. With your survey and leadership teams, choose a few key takeaways to address. As a leader, you will need to discern which points can be shared publicly and which are best addressed discreetly. Be as transparent as you can but as confidential as is prudent.

3. **Do something now.**
   People trust those who take quick action on issues. Too often, people stall while waiting for a "better opportunity," and they end up never taking any action at all. Don't spend too much time deciding or arguing about which priority should be done first. If it is hard to decide between two top priorities, move forward on

either one, and you will have more success because you acted on *something*. Always communicate what is being done. Quick, good action unleashes positive momentum. Momentum builds more momentum!

4. Overcommunicate.

We frequently think people understand what we're trying to say, but there's always more room for error than we imagine. You almost can't be clear enough especially amidst change or volatility. Take the time at each update to distill the important points into mission-aligned, succinct messages. People's minds start easily filling in the cracks if you leave too much to interpretation. Communicate in multiple formats and from multiple voices for your best chance at everyone fully absorbing what needs to be understood.

5. Make and keep your commitment.

Don't make a commitment you are not close to certain you will keep. As part of our Enterprise Trust Index™, we help senior leaders make commitments within two timeframes:

- Commit to taking action on three key priorities within 90 days. (You can *do* more, but only *commit* to three.)

- Commit to taking three more actions within the year.

We have found that senior leaders don't have to do *everything* people want, but if they keep those six commitments in those timeframes, trust goes up enormously. Every time you keep a commitment, be sure it is visible to others, so they can celebrate it and see that you do what you say you will do.

TRUST MATTERS

CLARITY

COMPASSION

CHARACTER

COMPETENCY

COMMITMENT

CONNECTION

CONTRIBUTION

CONSISTENCY

SOLVE WITH TRUST

6. Update with progress reports.

Without a plan for checking in on the key actions identified, your organization will find it difficult to know if any implementations have taken root. Follow the survey response plan and communicate how things are going. Without accountability, employees don't tend to trust; with it, people gain confidence that their actions matter and generate results.

7. Know what "done" looks like.

While progress is ongoing, you and your people may need to celebrate the end of the survey response process. Note what was accomplished, what has become standard practice, and what may still be addressed at a future time. Acknowledge who is carrying the responsibility of any ongoing changes. Then let it go and be done.

Best Practices

☐ Form a survey team to help put legs under all the communication and extra energy needed to process and implement change.

☐ Block off time for making a survey response plan that will take advantage of all the information.

☐ Create a survey response plan that spans three to six months including progress check-ins.

☐ Consider creating an additional survey website or page that employees can access updates on the purpose, timelines, and next steps of the process.

TRUST MATTERS

CLARITY

COMPASSION

CHARACTER

COMPETENCY

COMMITMENT

CONNECTION

CONTRIBUTION

CONSISTENCY

SOLVE WITH TRUST

> *Stop making strategy
> so hard.* —DH

Trust Tool #6: MVP™

Mission, Values, and *Priorities* can serve as powerful guides when used properly. While top leaders know these three guiding precepts are important, it's easy to operate day-to-day without thinking much about them. The advantage of having a defined mission, values, and key priorities is only realized if they are top-of-mind and followed. It would be like trying to get people to obey a constitution that is not upheld in the judicial system. Know why your mission is your mission, revisit your values often, and involve your people in the process of determining priorities.

MISSION

VALUES

PRIORITIES

Working with the MVP Model will help you get clear about the three most important areas of strategic clarity. Strategic plans can be overwhelming, wordy, and forgettable. When you make sure people know and understand what your MVP means to them, alignment and positive outcomes have a chance.

We will go deeper into parts of MVP in future tools but as an overview, the three important components are

- *Mission:* WHY your organization exists,

- *Values:* The WAY you operate and make decisions, and

- *Priorities:* Defining HOW you will accomplish your mission within your values.

The goal of using this model is to help your employees understand, agree on, and use your company's defined mission, values, and priorities to most effectively propel their work forward.

To decide who to involve in the defining of these terms for your company, consider what voices need to be heard, how you will get buy-in from all stakeholders, and how long you can work to finalize it. Some make it a very public process, some involve only top leadership, while others invite managers representing departments across the company to participate.

M – Mission

Mission is the highest purpose of your organization—the WHY—and will remain relatively unchanging. The mission usually starts with "To..." Our mission at TELI is "To develop trusted leaders and organizations." When we fulfill that mission, we believe we are helping people the most, because when trust increases, so does success, influence, and impact. Is your mission succinct and memorable? Does it get at the core of why you exist as an organization or team? Once you've settled on a mission statement, it should be reiterated often enough by all levels that every employee remembers what it is and understands how it applies to what they are doing.

TRUST MATTERS

CLARITY

COMPASSION

CHARACTER

COMPETENCY

COMMITMENT

CONNECTION

CONTRIBUTION

CONSISTENCY

SOLVE WITH TRUST

V – Values

Values depict the WAY you do things. By determining the way your organization will operate and make decisions, you are defining your boundaries. How far will you go to get a sale? What will you do to support the needs of your employees? How do you prioritize new products or initiatives? How do you make decisions here? When organizations have a clear set of values that everyone can remember and act on, decision-making gets quicker and more congruent throughout the organization. (See Trust Tool #13: Decision-Making Values in the Character Pillar.)

P – Priorities

Priorities keep you focused on next steps according to both the mission and the values. What are the most important items you should be focused on to accomplish your mission right now? I call them "push-forward priorities" or PFPs. They define how you will guide your actions forward in the current or upcoming period of time to accomplish your mission while being mindful of your values. It's crucial everyone understands which priorities will drive the company *forward*. I agree with the idea that you should not have more than three push-forward priorities at any given time. (See Trust Tool #7: Priority Alignment in the Clarity Pillar.)

Don't think your organization is too complex or too big to only have three priorities. I watched a big, international company of 400,000 employees successfully identify three push-forward priorities every month and share them consistently. What clarity!

Mission

Our mission is to:

_____

Values

We will make decisions based on these values:

1. _____

2. _____

3. _____

4. _____

5. _____

Priorities

Our top three push-forward priorities for the next 90 days:

1. _____

2. _____

3. _____

*This helped create alignment for one of the
biggest companies in the world.* ‑DH

Trust Tool #7: PRIORITY ALIGNMENT™

If your company priorities are ABC, then everyone's tasks
should be working toward some combination of A, B, or C and
never D, E, or F. Someone might be tasked with spending 100%
of their time on A, but they are still moving the company's
priorities forward. Another employee might be spending their
time on B and C, and so forth.

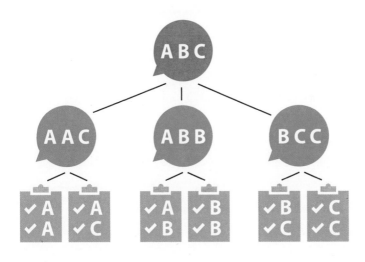

COMPETENCY

COMMITMENT

CONNECTION

CONTRIBUTION

CONSISTENCY

SOLVE WITH TRUST

Keeping priorities aligned across an entire organization takes thoughtful, strategic planning and constant communication. Limit your top push-forward priorities to three. Think you can't? I've seen some of the biggest companies in the world narrow their priorities from as many as 50 down to three. It's been shown time and time again, if a person has more than three key priorities, they can't enjoy optimal focus and may as well have no priorities at all.

Top priorities need to be shared at least every 90 days. One fast-growth tech company I worked with shared their top priorities every single week to get continual alignment, and it worked for them.

Create Company-wide Alignment

This concept is easy to understand but harder to accomplish. We suggest the following:

1. Start with a clear mission and values. (See Trust Tool #6: MVP for help on this.)

2. Communicate your mission and values widely and consistently.

3. In strategic planning, identify the push-forward priorities for the next 90 days or less.

4. Define how each department and person contributes to those priorities.

5. Communicate these priorities as frequently as necessary for all to begin internally noticing how their role aligns.

6. Examine any tasks or energy that is spent outside of those priorities.

7. Redistribute resources, tasks, and energy expenditures to point toward the top three priorities.

8. Re-examine, re-define, and re-share your top priorities at least every 90 days.

9. Continue communicating, celebrating, reporting on, and measuring by your top three priorities.

A president of a global organization once told me he knew he was achieving alignment when he heard the echo of their top priorities across all teams around the world. Now that's alignment! Your goal is the same: *create an echo.*

CLARITY

COMPASSION

CHARACTER

COMPETENCY

COMMITMENT

CONNECTION

CONTRIBUTION

CONSISTENCY

SOLVE WITH TRUST

TRUST MATTERS

Trust Tool #8: HOW? HOW? HOW?™

The three questions that actually take an idea to an action are How? How? How? If you don't know how you will get where you want to go, then *what* you are doing, *who* you are doing it with, or *why* you are doing it becomes meaningless. You might need to drill down by asking How? more times than you'd expect. **The key is to not stop until you've defined something specific you can act on today or tomorrow.** In the final How?, there should always be a *who, when,* and *where*. When you get to something you can do immediately, it gives hope!

HOW?   HOW?   HOW?

For example, if I intend to work-out tomorrow morning but don't commit to a specific time *when* I will work out, such as six a.m., chances are good that I won't get up on time. If I don't pre-decide *where* I will work out, such as the fitness center or running on the trail, the chance of success is lower. A How? How? How? plan will help you not revert to the default of staying in bed. From the manufacturing floor to a board room dilemma to setting goals, this strategy is something you can use all day, every day.

Who is often simply yourself in a personal goal. When creating plans with a team, make sure to assign each to-do to one specific person. Our research shows when there is more than one person on a final task, you have a 50% less chance of that task being completed. Instead of saying "Evan and Julie report back September 1," pick either Evan or Julie to own the project reporting, even if they work together.

Using the How? How? How? Tool

Determine the goal: _____

How am I going to get there? _____

How am I going to do that? _____

More specifically, how? _____

    Who will do it? _____

    When will they do it? _____

    Where will they do it? _____

I can't tell you how many people think they have this concept down, but once they try it, they realize it's going to take practice. You really have to ask How? How? How? repeatedly until you can drill down to something very specific that can be done today or tomorrow to achieve the desired outcome.

TRUST MATTERS

CLARITY

COMPASSION

CHARACTER

COMPETENCY

COMMITMENT

CONNECTION

CONTRIBUTION

CONSISTENCY

SOLVE WITH TRUST

Corporate Example

I worked with one of the biggest hospital groups in North America. We were at a private location with the top 100 leaders. After doing some trust work with great momentum and success, we uncovered more issues management needed to deal with quickly. I visited the table where the CEO was sitting.

I asked him, "What is needed the most in your organization?"

"A better culture," he replied.

"*How* could you start to have a better culture?"

"Clarity. We need more of that first pillar," he said.

"Great. *How* are you going to be clearer?"

"Communicate more."

"*How* will you communicate more?"

"We will hold each other accountable," he said.

"*How* will you hold each other accountable?"

I kept asking How? How? How? until the CEO (and each leader in the room) came up with something they could start doing right away to increase clarity and improve their culture. Years later, that CEO came back to me and confirmed that day was the tipping point for their organization becoming more cohesive, connected, and successful. I love to hear updates like this!

Personal Example

About a decade ago, my doctor said I needed to lose some weight (50 pounds). I had paid little attention to the pounds that had crept up on me, but I knew I needed to do something about my health. I started asking healthy-looking friends of mine what they did to stay in shape. Four words came back to me over and over: "Eat less; exercise more." I understood they were generally correct, but it wasn't clear enough to me yet. I knew I needed to take in less calories, but it was the How? How? How? process that helped me ***actually*** DO it.

Here's my personal How? How? How? example for taking in less calories:

My goal: Lose weight.

How? Take in fewer calories.

How? Stop ordering Coke when I travel (200 flights/year).

How? Order a calorie-free Fresca or water.

> *Who?* Me.

> *When?* During ALL travel.

> *Where?* Every flight. Every layover. Every restaurant.

My success at this change gave me momentum to eventually choose Fresca or water everywhere, every day. The How? How? How? process played a big role in changing my life and my health! It's important to get to something you can *and* will do. I wasn't going to start running marathons, but I could switch to Fresca!

Many people are so accustomed to setting vague goals that give zero hope. Repeatedly asking yourself How? may feel awkward at first but give it a try. Keep asking How? until you have a very specific and measurable action you will take. The good news is the final How? leaves you with a plan that propels you into motion.

To watch a video where I share more about the How? How? How? Trust Tool, visit TrustMattersBook.com/How.

Trust Tool #9: 90-DAY QUICK PLAN™

Now that you understand the How? How? How? Trust Tool, let's see how it's embedded in this more comprehensive strategic planning tool: the 90-Day Quick Plan.

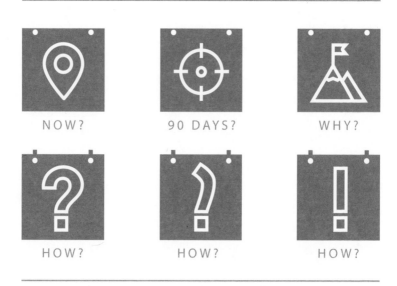

| NOW? | 90 DAYS? | WHY? |
| HOW? | HOW? | HOW? |

A common thought perpetuated by psychologists for decades was that you could create a new habit in 21 days, but we've come to realize that it is simply too short of a window of time for most change. We believe it takes about three months—or 90 days—to establish new patterns of behavior and accomplish an objective. James Clear, author of *Atomic Habits* says this longer timeline helps "us realize that habits are a process and not an event...You have to embrace the process. You have to commit to the system."[22]

Interestingly, more time doesn't necessarily get better results. The reason New Year's resolutions don't work for most people is because a year is actually too *much* time![23] Ninety days is short enough to stay focused but long enough to get more done than most people get done in a year. With commitment and consistency, we've seen the 90-Day Quick Plan change lives.

Create Your Plan

To create a 90-Day Quick Plan, answer these questions about a goal you have.

1. Where am I right now?

What is your starting point on this goal? If you don't know where you are at present, it will be difficult to gain direction on where you want to go in the future. If you want to have more sales, calculate your current sales numbers this week. If you want to run a marathon, ask, "How far can I already run today?" If you want to have a better relationship with your teenager, consider which topics are currently safe or divisive.

2. Where do I want to be in 90 days?

Where do you want to be with your goal in 90 days? Perhaps you want to run a marathon in a year but can currently only run one mile without stopping. Maybe your

TRUST MATTERS

CLARITY

COMPASSION

CHARACTER

COMPETENCY

COMMITMENT

CONNECTION

CONTRIBUTION

CONSISTENCY

SOLVE WITH TRUST

90-Day Quick Plan would entail being able to run seven miles without stopping. The bigger the goal, the more necessary it is to break it down into 90-day increments.

3. Why is this important to me?

The *why* is the motivation to stick with it, get to your destination, accomplish your goal, and see your priority attained. Clearly identifying your *why* helps you gain a deeper understanding, and appreciation for, the goal you've set in the first place as well as the results you expect to achieve. Now it's time for the How? How? How? process you already know!

> ❝
> We've been using the 90-Day Quick Plan consistently for our business unit's top priorities and are seeing the clarity really pay off in execution by our teams.
>
> —**Kristy Beckman**, VP, H.B. Fuller
> ❞

4. How am I going to do that?

What needs to happen before you can reach your goal? If you don't know how you will get where you want to go, then what you are doing becomes meaningless. Remember, having a HOW that you are willing to act on gives hope.

5. How am I going to do that?

Given your above answer, how would you accomplish that new thing?

6. How am I going to do that?

Given your above answer, how would you accomplish that new thing? Keep repeating this question until you can land on an answer that includes something that can be done by one person either today or tomorrow.

The 90-Day Quick Plan

Determine the goal: _____

Where am I currently with this goal? _____

Where do I want to be in 90 days? _____

Why is this important to me? _____

How am I going to do that? _____

How am I going to do that? _____

How am I going to do that? _____

  Who will do it? _____

  When will they do it? _____

  Where will they do it? _____

Clarity wins!

Bonus Resource: OneVoice Framework

Want another powerful clarity resource? The Trust Edge OneVoice Framework takes a strategic plan down to a one-page document and helps establish unity, alignment, and speed in messaging, decisions, and crisis. I have found when people get clear on the right key things, a huge percentage of potential problems are avoided. OneVoice includes a few of the Trust Tools taught in this book, but is more comprehensive than I have space for here. For the complete OneVoice Framework visit TrustMattersBook.com/OneVoice.

TRUST MATTERS

CLARITY

COMPASSION

CHARACTER

COMPETENCY

COMMITMENT

CONNECTION

CONTRIBUTION

CONSISTENCY

SOLVE WITH TRUST

Caring
matters.

TRUST MATTERS

CLARITY

COMPASSION

CHARACTER

COMPETENCY

COMMITMENT

CONNECTION

CONTRIBUTION

CONSISTENCY

SOLVE WITH TRUST

Pillar 2: Compassion

People put faith in those who care beyond themselves.

"WHO IS THE MOST TRUSTED person in the world?" By far, the single most common answer in our *Trust Outlook*® was "Mom." Why? It's because people trust those who put the interests of others ahead of their own, and with rare exception, that's what mothers do. Intent beyond yourself is a big part of compassion. Caring about the whole person—the motivation to act on someone else's behalf—is humankind at its best.

Compassion is not just "nice." It's a global human need that affects *every* bottom line. It's more than purely an interpersonal habit or priority. It is a value recognized and appreciated in every culture. Of all the pillars, Compassion can turn around some of your toughest challenges.

Why Does Compassion Matter?

- **People won't trust you if they don't see that you care beyond yourself.** Let people see by your actions, not just your words, that you care.

- **Compassion is contagious.** People who are well cared for care well for others.

- **People who feel cared for contribute more and stay with the company longer.** A compassionate culture stimulates innovation and problem solving while increasing job satisfaction, productivity, and resilience.

- **People need to be seen and understood.** In societies where we are becoming more isolated, compassion speaks loudly.

Compassion in the Workplace

Do not underestimate the power of compassion in the workplace. Caring about others can mean bringing a meal to a neighbor in need, but it can also look like knowing when to give a colleague some privacy, how to handle a missed deadline, or decreasing stimulation when a coworker is struggling with a migraine. Our humanness doesn't turn off when we step into the office.

An Ernst & Young, LLP survey of more than 1,000 U.S. employees confirmed that mutual empathy between company leaders and employees contributed to inspiring positive change within the workplace. The same survey found that 87% of U.S. workers believe empathetic leadership promotes higher job satisfaction.[24] Who doesn't want to be held accountable by a compassionate leader? Empathy really is a good business practice.

Compassion in the workplace is more than an interpersonal priority, however. Increasingly, in our interconnected world, it is a global value. Every year, people are finding it harder to trust companies that don't demonstrate they care about society, the environment, the disadvantaged, or the world at large. Whether internally, or externally, if you show you care beyond yourself, you will become trusted by those who follow you.

Compassion Broadens Perspective

Caring is founded in the ability to imagine someone else's situation. When we do that repeatedly, we expand our overall perspective. Not only can I relate to you better or act with more compassion, but my worldview is also now broader. Thinking with a mindset of compassion moves us to appreciate diverse perspectives.

Compassion Naturally Cascades

Some business leaders think caring for their *customers* is sufficient for success, but if *employees* don't feel cared about, it almost never trickles down to customers. Several years ago, when Delta Airlines wasn't doing well due to years of cost cutting and resulting low morale, they lost both loyal customers and market share. How did they turn things around? At the core, it wasn't a better frequent flyer program that focused on the customer. Instead, Delta started treating their *own* employees better. This led to happier team members who then treated their customers better. Delta Airlines has been among the top U.S. airlines ever since.[25]

TRUST MATTERS

CLARITY

COMPASSION

CHARACTER

COMPETENCY

COMMITMENT

CONNECTION

CONTRIBUTION

CONSISTENCY

SOLVE WITH TRUST

Just Love 'Em

Years ago, when I started presenting at large conferences I would often feel nervous and sometimes sick to my stomach as I waited backstage for my turn to speak. My wife, Lisa, did something incredible for me during those early years. She would put her hands on my shoulders and say, "Just love them. They can tell when you love them." It was what I needed to get my mind off my talking points and desire to be liked. It changed my focus from ME to THEM, allowing me to love and serve the audience to the best of my ability.

After more than 20 years of full-time speaking and consulting, Lisa *still* sends me texts right before keynotes or high-pressure consulting situations: "Just love 'em. They can tell when you love them."

It's Good for You

People who give of themselves end up receiving. You may or may not start seeing other people being kind back to you. What we CAN guarantee is that acting on the behalf of others will directly benefit you. People who kindly give to others feel better about themselves and typically have a more positive demeanor. In fact, the prestigious Mayo Clinic describes three big benefits of volunteering:

1. It improves physical and mental health.

2. It provides a sense of purpose and nurtures relationships.

3. It leads to an increase in lifespan.[26]

Don't delegate compassion work to other team members. If you do, you will miss out on the power it has to improve *your* life.

Agreement Isn't Required

People like to be around those they are like and agree with, but you don't have to agree with someone to be kind to them. Lately, I've had the privilege of serving as Senior Advisor to a bipartisan congressional group in Washington D.C. Believe it or not, there are members of Congress, both Democrats and Republicans, who want to work together! Unfortunately, there are many roadblocks to trust—ways our government even incentivizes distrust—that keep these leaders from making as much progress as they would like. What is most impressive about this bipartisan group is their willingness to set aside personal agendas and titles and rally around the many things they DO agree on.

My wise, older brother noted, "We are in a more critical world than ever before, without the ability to critically think." Harsh judgment with little compassion is commonplace today. Leaders, you are going to get critiqued no matter what! Be a part of the solution by avoiding the divisive games, building up your own character, focusing on the good you see, and expressing gratitude for it. If members of Congress can come together, we can too!

> Compassion toward those
> who are different than you
> is true compassion.

TRUST MATTERS

CLARITY

COMPASSION

CHARACTER

COMPETENCY

COMMITMENT

CONNECTION

CONTRIBUTION

CONSISTENCY

SOLVE WITH TRUST

A Sense of Security Enables Productivity

One of the greatest challenges of leadership is to create an environment that is conducive to meaningful work relationships and overall success. When people feel unsafe—psychologically, physically, or otherwise—the natural response is to spend energy on protecting or guarding themselves.

The American Psychological Association found that "nine out of 10 employees in the U.S. want their employer to value their emotional and psychological welfare—and to provide relevant support."[27] When people feel safe and valued, they are willing to share new ideas, give constructive criticism, and deliver generous praise. This healthier environment leads to increased innovation, productivity, and trust.

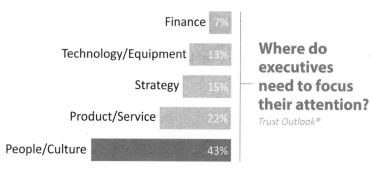

Finance 7%
Technology/Equipment 13%
Strategy 15%
Product/Service 22%
People/Culture 43%

Where do executives need to focus their attention?
Trust Outlook®

Higher engagement scores are the natural outcome of a high-trust culture.

Retention and Contribution

Whether at work or in friendship, people who feel cared for stay longer. SIY Global confirms, "People on your team want to know that you want them to succeed. You've got their back. Their professional and personal development is part of your agenda. Knowing that you have their best interests at heart is a key motivating piece."[28] When employees feel that their leaders and colleagues genuinely care about them, they are more likely to be top contributors in the company!

COMPASSION TRUST TOOLS

#10 **LAWS of Compassion**

#11 **SPA Appreciation**

#12 **PAWS in Conflict**

TRUST MATTERS

CLARITY

COMPASSION

CHARACTER

COMPETENCY

COMMITMENT

CONNECTION

CONTRIBUTION

CONSISTENCY

SOLVE WITH TRUST

> *Just focusing on the "W" of this tool*
> *can change every interaction.* ⌐DN

Trust Tool #10: LAWS OF COMPASSION™

How do we show compassion? Listen, Appreciate, Wake up, and Serve (LAWS). These are guidelines for demonstrating that you care. The more you practice operating like this, the more natural it becomes.

LISTEN   **W**AKE UP!

APPRECIATE   **S**ERVE

Use these four positive habits to build capacity and awareness for compassion in the home and workplace.

L – Listen

In our fast-paced, attention-span-deprived culture, it's easy to become distracted. Bad listening habits aren't just rude; they are expensive. Good listening becomes a powerful tool for gaining trust.

One of the ways to demonstrate that we genuinely value others is to give them our undivided attention when they speak. That means we stop, make eye contact, be present, acknowledge their point of view, and don't interrupt or allow interruptions.

At my first job, I had a manager who was well-liked but not very high up in the company. One day, when I was giving him a progress update, an executive in the company walked up to us, expecting to tell my boss something that was on his mind.

My manager did something I'll never forget. He stayed facing toward me and kept focused on our conversation until we were finished. I couldn't believe it: as an intern, I completely expected our conversation to get interrupted! The ability to not be distracted and to keep the person in front of you as *most important* can make you unforgettable. I have not forgotten that experience 30 years later.

Another action you can do to help people feel cared for is to put away anything that would distract you. The unintended message you send is that you are not fully engaged with the person in front of you. Try not to have your phone or computer out during meetings. Shut off any potential notification sounds on a smart watch or phone, or else you and everyone else will be constantly distracted.

Pause to Reflect

❓ *How well am I doing at listening to my friends, family and colleagues?*

❓ *Consider asking others who know you well to give you feedback on your listening habits.*

TRUST MATTERS

CLARITY

COMPASSION

CHARACTER

COMPETENCY

COMMITMENT

CONNECTION

CONTRIBUTION

CONSISTENCY

SOLVE WITH TRUST

A – Appreciate

In our global study, we found that the #1 reason people leave an organization was *not feeling appreciated*. William Arthur Ward said, "Feeling gratitude and not expressing it is like wrapping a present and not giving it."[29]

People tend to thrive when they are recognized for notable work. Make a habit of acknowledging people's intentions, efforts, and meaningful contributions. This does not mean to tell everyone "good job" when they didn't do a good job.

What it does mean is when you notice someone making a meaningful contribution or doing something noteworthy, tell them so!

Do you have a recognition program? Can you make it easier for your people to create a culture of appreciation? My Chief of Staff places thank-you notes on the middle of the board room table for our weekly staff meetings to encourage people to pick one up and write a note.

> **"**
> After putting the LAWS of Compassion into action, it quickly became our favorite. Simply put, the customer must come first in everything we do. The result: a stellar quarter and year!
>
> **—Joe Raschke**, Business Value Advisor, Trust Edge Certified Partner
> **"**

Is it powerful? Absolutely. One leader we sent a thank-you card to years ago continues to recommend our work to some of the biggest companies in the world. Initially, he said he remembered us because of the handwritten thank-you card.

Pause to Reflect

❓ *Do I appreciate the good things around me every day?*

❓ *Consider making a list of ways you could offer acknowledgment to the people in your life.*

W – Wake up!

Be present. Be aware. Have you ever known someone who can make you feel like you're the only person who matters? Awareness is a skill you can develop. Practice walking into a room and quickly cataloging the emotions you read. Note if there is something you could do to show you care. Besides showing compassion, your awareness can sometimes save you from an embarrassing or awkward situation.

When you are AWAKE to the person in front of you, they can feel it. Today that is a uniquely powerful feeling. Author Maya Angelou said, "People will forget what you *said*, people will forget what you *did*, but people will never forget how you *made them feel*."[30]

Do you get frustrated when your children have their eyes on their screens or when you are talking to someone, and they look down at their smart watch? Most people do.

One simple thing you can do to *Wake up* and be present is to put away your phone. Dr. Frances Frei of Harvard Business School says. "If you do nothing else, please put away your phone. It is the largest distraction magnet yet to be made, and it is super difficult to create empathy and trust in its presence."[31] The unintended message is that you are not fully engaged.

Pause to Reflect

❓ *How did I do on noticing people's emotions or needs this week?*

❓ *Is there a particular person, group, or situation that could use my elevated awareness?*

S – Serve

It's human nature to prioritize your own goals and well-being. Practicing compassion doesn't mean you have to deny your own interests or become a martyr. It simply means growing an awareness for when to pause and shift perspective to others.

To serve means looking out for the interests of others and knowing when it's your opportunity to act on the compassion you feel. Grab lunch for someone in a hurry, help carry a heavy load to the car, notice when someone is having a bad day, and celebrate when other people have wins. Demonstrate a generous spirit. Volunteer. Be kind. It's good for you!

Pause to Reflect

❓ *Are there ways I have outgrown service in my own mind?*

❓ *Whose well-being could I attend to this week?*

TRUST MATTERS

CLARITY

COMPASSION

CHARACTER

COMPETENCY

COMMITMENT

CONNECTION

CONTRIBUTION

CONSISTENCY

SOLVE WITH TRUST

> *Be someone who appreciates
> others effectively.* ⌐DN

Trust Tool #11: SPA APPRECIATION™

Appreciation is underrated. Everyone longs to be recognized and appreciated for their hard work. This doesn't mean blue ribbons for all; it means that when you notice people doing something well and celebrate it *in a way that is meaningful to them*, a huge impact is made. Well executed appreciation can even increase your bottom line.

SPECIFIC   **P**ERSONAL   **A**UTHENTIC

Use the SPA Appreciation Trust Tool as a checklist for any-time you have an opportunity to recognize someone. In work cultures where appreciation is the norm, people both stay longer and work harder. It's easy to go through the motions of showing appreciation without having any real impact. Use SPA Appreciation to recognize a deserving individual in a way that will be both impactful and memorable.

Practicing SPA Appreciation

S – Specific

Specificity breeds credibility. To make your appreciation efforts impactful, ask yourself what exactly you are noticing that they have done well. Saying, "Good job" to someone is much less powerful than saying, "I noticed the extra hours, effort, and creativity you put into making this project a success." When thanking the host of a dinner party, instead of simply saying, "Thanks for the great party," it is more meaningful to notice something specific: "The way you encouraged everyone to participate meant a lot to me." Precisely craft your message around what set the person's effort apart. Specific praise is always better!

> **"**
> *The SPA Appreciation Trust Tool is for connecting with people in an authentic way. It is a simple way to start leading with more heart.*
> —**Patsy McFadden**, Organizational Development and Training Manager, City of Las Vegas (Ret.)
> **"**

P – Personal

It's easy to give recognition in the way *you* would want to receive it, but to be more effective, consider what type of recognition the individual you are thanking would prefer. A thoughtful gift or verbal acknowledgment? Public recognition or a nicely written card signed by everyone? Making it personal could mean using an accepted nickname, buying a favorite candy or coffee drink, or even celebrating at a favorite place or time that is meaningful to them. Making it personal is always worth the effort.

I once received a thank-you gift of some customized cuff links from a well-known pro-sports team I was working with. As I realized what the box contained, I was very surprised to see that they were not brandishing the organization's logo. Instead, they sent me fly-fishing-themed cuff links. Why? Because they knew I *love* to fly fish!

Wow, that thoughtfulness meant a lot to me! To this day, when I wear my fly-fishing cuff links, I smile and think of that team positively. When you find out a colleague's favorite dessert and remember to bring it during the week of their birthday, they feel cared about beyond expectation. Personalizing whenever possible can make a huge difference.

Insincere appreciation is worse than no appreciation.

A – Authentic

Whether praising your employee in a public setting or in an appreciation note, make sure your efforts come across as authentic and genuine. Motivation often follows appreciation. It isn't the direct reason why you take the time to authentically appreciate, but it is definitely one of the positive outcomes! The feeling that you get when your are genuinely appreciated is unmatched!

A memorable story about an unfortunate lack of authenticity comes from a friend of mine. He once developed an innovative system that saved his company enormous amounts of time and money. During the next regular staff meeting, his manager nonchalantly slid a little cardboard box over to him. Inside the box was the generic corporate gift the company always used for recognition. Nothing was said verbally, making the whole event feel awkward and insincere. He soon left the company and started his own competitive business. Take this as a cautionary tale: whatever you choose to do, do it authentically. People can tell if you mean it or not.

TRUST MATTERS

CLARITY

COMPASSION

CHARACTER

COMPETENCY

COMMITMENT

CONNECTION

CONTRIBUTION

CONSISTENCY

SOLVE WITH TRUST

Appreciate Well with SPA

Take the time to practice **S**pecific, **P**ersonal, and **A**uthentic appreciation; I guarantee you will experience a positive change in trust when you do.

☐ **S** = Are your methods or words *specific* to an individual's efforts?

☐ **P** = Are your methods or words *personalized* to the individual?

☐ **A** = Is your delivery *authentic*?

Motivation follows appreciation.

TRUST MATTERS

CLARITY

COMPASSION

CHARACTER

COMPETENCY

COMMITMENT

CONNECTION

CONTRIBUTION

CONSISTENCY

SOLVE WITH TRUST

> *Conflict is inevitable. Follow these for success in tough conversations.* ‑DH

Trust Tool #12: PAWS IN CONFLICT™

The PAWS in Conflict Trust Tool stands for **P**osture, **A**ctions, **W**ords, and **S**olution. It helps keep (or even build) trust during times of conflict. Some leaders really struggle with facing conflict. Others create conflict without even realizing what they are doing. No matter your situation, improving these key skills will create greater trust in tough interactions. In fact, one of your opportunities to build trust the fastest is *in the middle* of conflict. It's how you respond that matters.

| **P**OSTURE | **A**CTIONS | **W**ORDS | **S**OLUTION |

According to a 2022 Myers-Briggs report, the average number of hours per week an employee spends dealing with workplace conflict is "4.34 hours per week." Over a third of employees said they deal with conflict often.[32] Approaching conflict with a compassionate mindset, looking to understand the other point of view, can often dissolve much of the problem. Without compassion, you can't have healthy accountability, alignment, or unity in your organization.

Conflict is inevitable, but you can deal with it in a way that builds trust.

P – Posture

When you view conflict as inevitable and necessary for improvement, you can approach it more proactively. Use safe and welcoming body language. Some studies say up to 90% of communication is non-verbal.

One way to reduce defensiveness is by entering a potentially tense conversation with an open posture (open hands, arms to the sides, body facing the other person and leaning in, attention steady but comfortable). Where you situate yourself in the room matters too. If possible, sit next to or on the same side of the table. This co-sharing of space can bring down the tension and help create the mindset that you are in this together.

It can be wise to block time before the meeting to reset your mind and posture especially if that day has already been intense or rushed. Make sure there is no technology such as a mobile device or computer screen between you.

Quiet mirroring can be an effective posture. If they stand, you stand. If they sit, you sit. This equals out the power: just don't mirror an angry tone and energy. Be curious, try to understand the person's story and point of view, and most of all, be in an attentive and listening posture in your mind as well as your body.

A – Active listening

In conflict situations, prepare for active listening. Asking curious and clarifying questions can lead the conversation in a healthy way. Repeat back what you hear to ensure the other perspective is understood and there is agreement on what is being discussed. Suspend judgment and listen for potential motivations and biases which can lead you to solutions. If the situation is potentially volatile, it's usually best to stay in investigator mode but don't match their intensity. It's a lot harder to keep the "fight" going when the other person is the only one fighting.

For me, patience is hard, but I've found it is critical in tense situations and can have a dramatic effect on outcomes. At my best, I like to consider the life experience behind the other person's words rather than queuing up what I will say in return as soon as they take a breath. Don't interrupt. Wait. This can be challenging if the conversation is long or the topic is uncomfortable, but allowing the person time to develop their thoughts can avoid defensiveness and actually bring a resolution more quickly.

Conflict is an opportunity to grow!

W – Words

Make wise choices with your words. Be generous with your words. There can be particular words you *should* or *shouldn't* use. Avoid saying anything that does not need to be said. If it isn't true, helpful, or kind, don't say it! Use "I" language instead of accusatory "you" language. Try, "I feel frustrated when _____" rather than, "You made me_____." Unyielding words like *always* and *never* destroy credibility.

TRUST MATTERS

CLARITY

COMPASSION

CHARACTER

COMPETENCY

COMMITMENT

CONNECTION

CONTRIBUTION

CONSISTENCY

SOLVE WITH TRUST

In an effort to de-escalate and make peace, some people can be tempted to stop communicating clearly. Have the courage to uphold truth *and* use discernment to know when to speak and when to listen. A few more phrases that might help in conflict are:

1. "So what I'm hearing is...."

2. "Help me understand your point of view."

3. "Thank you for sharing; is there anything else?"

4. "I think our perspectives are different. What we seem to agree on is...."

S – Solution

Plan for improvement and always be forward focused. Don't get caught up emotionally. Practice the discipline of keeping ALL the conversation focused on the issue at hand. The blame game kills trust and blocks resolution.

Use language that keeps you focused on the solution such as, "What are some possible remedies or win-wins for this situation?" or "What would you propose that would help solve this challenge?" In a particularly intense interaction, it is often a viable option to decide to reconvene at another time.

With compassion, it is common to come through an intense interaction and actually build trust. When people see that you really want to understand their perspective, your credibility goes up, and you can take a step closer to a deeper, more trusted relationship. Add the pillars of connection and character, and you have a winning combination for building trust in conflict.

Never underestimate the power of compassion.

Doing what's right matters.

TRUST MATTERS

CLARITY

COMPASSION

CHARACTER

COMPETENCY

COMMITMENT

CONNECTION

CONTRIBUTION

CONSISTENCY

SOLVE WITH TRUST

Pillar 3: Character

People notice those who do what is right over what is easy.

CLEARLY, STRONG CHARACTER is a crucial ingredient of trust—inside and outside the workplace. While clarity and compassion demonstrate what you do and how you do it, character is all about who you are at your core. People who are strong in this pillar tend to act on principles rather than feelings. They act consistently despite their circumstances. In today's world, a leader's decisions are highly visible and easily scrutinized. Operating with high character safeguards against costly moral and financial disaster.

Why Character Matters

- ***Exercising high character builds trust in yourself.*** It is the foundation of all other trusted relationships. Your own history of right-over-easy choices builds the confidence and conviction to do it again.

- *Character helps you KEEP a culture of trust even amidst chaos.* The character of your people plays a crucial role in how well a company does in the face of adversity.

- *A culture of character is extremely attractive.* When an employer operates consistently and with integrity, people not only take notice but try to get hired there.

- *Moral failures are costly.* From banks to baseball players, it doesn't take long to see the personal, financial, and global impact of moral choices at the top.

- *Decisions made from values make life simpler and decision-making faster.* Predetermined principles takes the stress, guess work, and inconsistency out of making congruent choices.

Expectations Have Changed

I've noticed that parents often say to their kids when they are going out with friends, "Have fun!" I don't recall my parents saying that when I was a kid. I remember them saying, "Be good." Have we elevated pleasure over principle? In a *Fast Company* article, Tracy Brower said, "Better than pursuing fun for its own sake is having a compelling purpose for the work. Working on something that matters and being able to make a unique and significant contribution is more fulfilling than having a few entertaining moments with team members."[33]

In the long term, satisfaction is more fulfilling than pleasure. I may not be motivated to work out, but afterwards I always feel better both physically and mentally. Being good or doing what is right—having good character—leads to more enjoyment in life, and most importantly, builds trust in yourself.

Character Is Worth Building

When I taught Ethics at a university, it was clear, even across wide cultural and religious differences, that high character can be standardized and mostly agreed upon. No matter your experiences, your good or bad role models, or where you derive your values from, anyone can build their character muscles. Yale University affirms, when people see that you are reliable, authentic, respectful, consistent, humble, ethical, and full of integrity, they will be more inclined to engage with you, work with you, lend a hand to you, talk positively about you, and in general, *trust* you.[34]

With intentionality, you can grow
and strengthen your character!

Character Is a Goldmine
in the Workplace

Character is not only critical to lead your current teams, but it's also essential in hiring trustworthy employees. The 2023 Bentley-Gallup Business in Society Report found that an overwhelming 93% of job seekers say it is important to work for a company that makes money in ways that are ethical. In order to attract the best candidates for your organization, strength of character becomes both a personal and professional advantage.[35]

Public education widely recognizes that a student environment should promote good sense and positive virtues.

Likewise, leading companies are now spending close to a third of their learning and development budget on soft skills development because they know it drives positive outcomes.[36]

Would YOU Follow You?

Early in my career, I was invited to be the opening keynote for a leadership conference with some much bigger name speakers: experts that I really looked up to. The most disappointing part of my experience was spending time backstage with the other presenters and noticing that a few of them acted differently off-stage than on. Of course, no one is perfect, but that experience led my company to create this as one of our values: *seek to be the same off-stage as on-stage.*

Everyone has a platform of influence whether it is personal relationships, social media, or a literal stage!

With the amplification of influencers in recent years, we all have a front row seat to examples of poor and weak character. Whenever the motivation for money or influence is greater than the desire for character, longevity becomes precarious. It's easy to become blind to our own inconsistencies. I have needed to rely on others to help me see opportunities for character growth. High-character leaders cultivate accountability, crave feedback, and seek mentorship. We need people who care about us enough to give us the truth.

Here are several ways to pursue personal accountability:

- Self-reflection can be as simple as asking yourself: *Would I have followed my own leadership this week?* It's also good to get away from time to time and honestly reflect on how you are doing.

- Ask a trusted friend or mentor to give you specific feedback on how you're coming across. What motivations do they see you operating under?

- Consider a 360° assessment that will help you detect character gaps that can be acted on. These types of assessments help with self-awareness and are most valuable if you have a coach or trusted colleague to talk it through. (Visit MeasureMyTrust.com to see recommended assessments.)

Incentivizing For or Against Character

As a leader of a team, home, or organization, you are the culture keeper! You are incentivizing higher or lower character everyday by what you laugh at, what actions you allow to take place, who you listen to, and the reward systems you create (or allow). I watched a pro sports team that incentivized so much sarcasm that the humor lost its humor and turned into poison. In the end, it affected their on-field performance and cost them playoff wins.

The 2016 Wells Fargo banking scandal is an example of managers incentivizing character they didn't want to see. Encouraging unrealistic sales goals resulted in some of their bankers opening millions of false accounts from 2002–2016 in customers' names without their knowledge.[37] The U.S. Department of Justice announced in February 2022 that Wells Fargo had to pay $3 billion as a penalty for this offense.[38] They could have prevented this loss of public trust if they had examined the internal incentives offered to their bankers and made changes to better reflect their values. Be careful what you incentivize!

> ## Hold on to your integrity and moral compass.

Safeguard Your Leadership

We've all seen complete and utter moral failures in the news. What these tragic stories have in common is a small, bad decision that spiraled into a large-scale, awful situation. A breach of character is not only financially expensive, but it can also end businesses and destroy lives. Making choices about how you will act before you hit a temptation to compromise can save you from the slippery slope.

We all want to live proactively instead of reactively. Determine that you will make decisions based on the values and principles you want to live by. Pre-deciding based on something you believe in makes life simpler and more peaceful.

> ## Live a proactive life.

I consulted for some time with a senior leadership team at one of the biggest companies in the world. We'd seen progress, but their management team still had issues. They didn't have a problem coming to a consensus; they had a problem with a senior leader who would not stay committed to the decisions they made as a team. After a group decision, individuals would privately come to this leader with various opinions and ideas they neglected to share in the team meeting, and he would end up changing his mind on the issue. This undermined the senior leadership team's decisions, and it was quickly becoming a toxic situation.

Something had to be done. Together, we created a list of five values that the senior leadership team could commit to. The most helpful value agreed upon that day was: "We will discuss, debate, decide, and then leave our meeting defending the decision with one voice." I needed to help this leader understand that pivoting on a decision was okay, but it absolutely *must* be done back in the room with the entire team where they would discuss, debate, decide, and leave the meeting defending the decision as one. It helped this leader, and the team as a whole, to stand strong when individuals came trying to privately persuade a change in the decision.

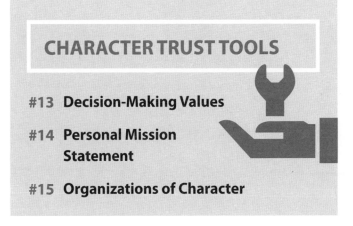

CHARACTER TRUST TOOLS

#13 Decision-Making Values

#14 Personal Mission Statement

#15 Organizations of Character

Trust Tool #13:
DECISION-MAKING VALUES™

The beauty of having a well-defined, pre-determined set of values
is that it makes your decisions faster, easier, and more consistent. A
set of values coupled with a commitment to follow them in every cir-
cumstance means that, in many situations, your decision is already
made for you. You'll increase your odds for success, and you'll sleep
better at night.

DECISION-MAKING VALUES

Personal Decision-Making Values

One way to increase the likelihood of living congruent to your
intentions is to identify a set of specific values you can consult as a
behavioral yardstick whenever you must make a decision of any consequence. Values are ways you operate and determine how you will

act. By choosing what's important to you, you draw boundary lines, helping you see what choices you will and won't make. For example:

- I will prioritize people over tasks.

- I will do what is right over what is easy.

- I will consider the long-term impact of a decision.

- I will have a bias for quality and excellence.

- I will honor the absent.

These can seem simple to say, but in order to keep them as priority, it's really important to know *why* you value them. If this is your first run at a set of personal values, you may want to spend some time uncovering your deeper motivations for these values. It's easy to rattle off things you think you value or know you should value, but to make a list of your actual values is harder. Once you have your values set, you may find there is a sequence of importance. If so, try numbering them and memorizing them.

Company Decision-Making Values

In the workplace, defining your Decision-Making Values moves you down the path to being trusted. You can do this in any team or company to align and speed up decision-making. All social groups develop norms, good or bad. By predetermining a specific set of values, work teams and organizations can frame productive norms that will bring the positive results they need to succeed. Companies that collectively commit to their top-five team values can significantly change their behavior, effectiveness, and efficiency.

If one of your Decision-Making Values is "Excellence in Service," then when selecting a venue for an event, you might choose the more expensive one if it allows you to serve your customer in a more excellent way. Our company value around providing excellence is the reason my printed books have only been hardcover. Decision-making gets faster and more consistent across the organization when decisions are made by agreed-upon values.

Values become reality when they truly guide our decisions.

A short phrase is often more tangible than a single abstract word. Here are some examples:

- We will provide excellence in service.
- We will show integrity in our actions.
- We will show ourselves to be trustworthy.
- We will display count-on-me character.
- We will speak in the best interest of those not present.
- We will respect each other's time.
- We will come to meetings prepared.
- We will treat others as we would like to be treated.

As with personal values, take time to explore *why* these are most important. In order to ensure alignment, we recommend deciding these values as a team and assigning a plan for communication and even role-modeling the process when you can. Remember, these are not just statements you agree on, these are the values you will make decisions by. Once you've battled it out, your values will be memorable, repeatable, and actionable.

Decision-Making Values Applied

In 1932, businessman Herbert J. Taylor was asked to take over a company facing bankruptcy. With way more owed to creditors than his assets were worth, he compelled every part of the organization to act by, make decisions by, and live by four questions. Taylor said he created them as questions because he didn't want to tell leaders what they should think or do. He wanted them to come to their own decisions. Taylor called it the "Four-Way Test." He soon had the company memorizing, sharing, training, and checking advertising copy against the Four-Way Test. What followed? Massive success![39]

Herbert J. Taylor was a member of the Rotary Club in Rhode Island, and his Four-Way Test was soon shared there. Rotarians across the country began reciting the Four-Way Test at every meeting and it continues to this day. See if this inspires you:

Rotary Four-Way Test
Of the things we think, say, or do...

1. *Is it the TRUTH?*

2. *Is it FAIR to all concerned?*

3. *Will it build GOODWILL and BETTER FRIENDSHIPS?*

4. *Will it be BENEFICIAL to all concerned?*[40]

As a leader, you make a myriad of important decisions every day; you want to be successful, *and* you want to encourage great character. Decide your personal or organizational values, then emphasize and repeat them until they're engrained enough to live by without thinking.

> *Do not underestimate the power of a Personal Mission Statement.* -DN

Trust Tool #14:
PERSONAL MISSION STATEMENT™

While a bucket list can be fun and inspiring, a mission statement can bring you deeper satisfaction. Living a life by design and on purpose gives you an opportunity to experience the greatest sense of fulfillment.

Create a Personal Mission Statement

One of the simplest ways to create a Personal Mission Statement is to imagine what you would want your obituary to say about how you lived your life. This exercise can be sobering and inspiring at the same time. Imagine what each of the following groups of people might say about you. Answer the questions below about what you *hope* certain people will say after you die:

1. What do you want your spouse/partner to remember about you?

2. What do you want your children/family to remember about you?

3. What do you want friends to remember about you?

4. What do you want coworkers to remember about you?

5. What do you want your community to remember about you?

6. What do you hope God would say about you?

TRUST MATTERS

CLARITY

COMPASSION

CHARACTER

COMPETENCY

COMMITMENT

CONNECTION

CONTRIBUTION

CONSISTENCY

SOLVE WITH TRUST

Now that you have these phrases jotted down, choose at least three of them and re-write them as your Personal Mission Statement beginning with the word *To*:

- Example 1: *My personal mission is to be dependable, positive, and full of integrity.*

- Example 2: *My personal mission is to be a proactive leader who anticipates the needs of my teams, to give my family my best self, and to take time to encourage those who are struggling.*

- Example 3: *My mission is to honor God and love every person I meet by being present, caring, and trustworthy.* (Is this one too personal? Nope! This is your *Personal* Mission Statement.)

Once you have written your first draft, take some time to think through it. Can you make it shorter or more accurate? Can you make it more actionable? Do you need to add something that is missing from your list of answers?

It's a Living Document

You've written a Personal Mission Statement, but how do you make sure it stays top of mind and a useful tool in your work and personal life?

1. Put your Personal Mission Statement in a place where you will see it often.

2. Read it regularly, preferably out loud.

3. Share it with an accountability partner or mentor.

4. Review it periodically. Examine it for areas of your life that have gotten out of alignment.

TRUST MATTERS

CLARITY

COMPASSION

CHARACTER

COMPETENCY

COMMITMENT

CONNECTION

CONTRIBUTION

CONSISTENCY

SOLVE WITH TRUST

> *A pathway to systemize*
> *high character.* ⌐DN⌐

Trust Tool #15:
ORGANIZATIONS OF CHARACTER™

Hiring and retaining people with good character can be challenging, but this tool is a great exercise to get you started. You may find you need to take extra time to truly define what character means in your organization. It will be important to have agreement on this because all the other steps will refer to it.

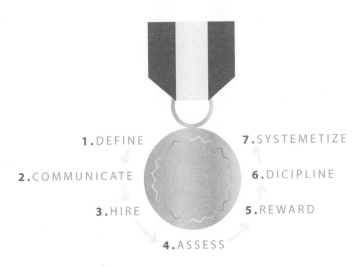

1. DEFINE   7. SYSTEMETIZE

2. COMMUNICATE   6. DICIPLINE

3. HIRE   5. REWARD

4. ASSESS

Emphasizing High Character

1. Define it.

What do you want high character to look like in your organization? I define character using morality and integrity because morals are nothing without consistency. For your specific group, agree on your own definition and identify the primary reasons why it matters in your daily work life and industry. Ideally, you will come up with a few specific examples of what high character looks like when it is seen in your organization. (TIP: Make sure to use Trust Tool #8: How? How? How? during this process.) It can be super helpful to use with this tool, making sure you get down to an action you can take right away. Here are some valuable character traits for the workplace. Use these to help you define character for your group:

Reliable	Patient	Self-Aware
Authentic	Compassionate	Fair
Respectful	Loyal	Self-Disciplined
Consistent	Honorable	Courageous
Humble	Self-Controlled	Selfless
Ethical	Wise	Conscientious
Full of Integrity	Discreet	Honest

2. Communicate it.

Promote your definition of character. Use language that assumes the best to avoid coming across as condescending. Stories of what character looks like can make it more understandable and actionable. In my company, a story is often told about a shipping person who drove all night to get our training toolkits to an event for senior leaders. That story has inspired us over and over to live out our character through both words and actions.

3. Hire on it.

Overlooking character in the hiring process is costly and dangerous. Embed your character definition and primary reasons it matters into your interview process. Include questions, especially in conversations with references, that point to the character traits your group values most.

The Trust Edge material has profoundly impacted my work. The implementation and strategic utilization of Trust Edge concepts has ushered in a new era of clarity and efficiency in my work with school districts. By instilling clear objectives, tangible timelines, and detailed clarifications, our work with school districts is much more productive. We are optimizing operational efficiency and have also fostered a culture of trust, collaboration, and innovation.

—**Aaron Sinclair**, Director of School Leadership, Sourcewell

4. Assess it.

As a part of your development process, measure for character. Don't just rely on gut feelings. Find ways to target the character traits that matter most to you in your review processes. We have tools at TELI that could help with this. Visit MeasureMyTrust.com to learn more.

5. Reward it.

The best companies don't just reward results, they reward high character. Often, character and achievement go hand in hand. Sometimes, exemplary character is on full display, and we miss it. Be ready to identify and celebrate high character. Several companies that have embedded the 8 Pillars of Trust into their culture give "Pillar Awards" to accentuate those who live out the Pillars well. In at least one company, the Character Award is considered the most prestigious.

6. Discipline it.

Act quickly when you see low character, so it doesn't infect the entire team or company. There must be some sort of correction if an employee fails to show the type of character that is expected of them. Refer to the company definitions of character and use discernment for how and when this will be best received. Low character must be coached and, if improvement isn't noticed, then removal may be the best, and even most compassionate, way to respond for all involved. Consider using Trust Tool #12: PAWS in Conflict in the Compassion Pillar.

7. Systemize it.

Consistently incentivize high character and avoid the lure of short-term results. Be in touch with the pressures being put on your employees at every level to make sure you're not accidentally incentivizing dishonesty or selfish behavior. People are motivated by expectations, rewards, what is talked about, how people are hired, promotions, and decision frameworks. Make sure your systems align with high character and work to create an environment where doing the right thing is the cultural norm.

Character creates credibility.

Abilities matter.

Pillar 4: Competency

People have confidence in those who stay fresh, relevant, and capable.

REMEMBER WHEN we wrote expressions like "You rock!" and "Stay the same!" in our friends' school yearbooks? What terrible advice! Please don't stay the same. Learn. Mature. Change. Get better.

We don't tend to trust people or organizations that stay the same in their area of expertise. We don't trust the leader who hasn't recently read a leadership book, the accountant who isn't up to date on the newest tax laws, or the computer engineer who is coding the same way they were five minutes ago. (Okay, maybe more than five minutes.) Individuals who have a strong Competency Pillar have a perpetual thirst for learning and understand that to stay fresh, relevant, and capable in their work, they must be intentional about it.

TRUST MATTERS

CLARITY

COMPASSION

CHARACTER

COMPETENCY

COMMITMENT

CONNECTION

CONTRIBUTION

CONSISTENCY

SOLVE WITH TRUST

Why Competency Matters

- *We are in a skills-based revolution.* From the use of ChatGPT to soft skills like resilience, shifts in the job market reveal the need for employees to upskill.

- *Ongoing learning is a must.* No degree can provide enough knowledge for a lifetime. Continuous learning is critical in this fast-paced working environment.

- *Learning and development opportunities keep employees.* I have seen the right training lower attrition and save millions of dollars.

- *Competent workers are more likely to innovate.* Strong skills development makes for capable people who have more ideas and energy to be creative.

Changing Expectations

Today, the key competency to learn is not a specific skill but rather *how* to learn and how to learn *fast*. In many industries like healthcare, there continues to be a move toward micro-specialization. In other industries, you might be expected to have a wide knowledge base across many subject areas. Added to that pressure is speed. We value speed of information, and we expect people to pick up new ideas and skills quickly. To be successful in many fields, there is a demand to stay up to speed on lightning-fast trends and tech advancements.

Input = Output

Every science affirms it: input always affects output! German physicist Rudolf Clausius discovered the First Law of Thermodynamics and is credited with making it a science to be studied. He found the energy you put in is exactly the same as the energy you get out.[41] In theology or agriculture this sounds like, "You reap what you sow." And in psychology, we know that the thoughts you put in your head lead to beliefs which lead to actions. In basic physiology, if you eat something that gives you food poisoning, well...input equals output!

If you want better output, stronger competency, or more capacity, you have to evaluate your input. If I put in workouts, I get out a better physique. If I put kindness and love into my marriage and friendships, I get healthier relationships. And it's the same with individuals and organizations. If I see a team or company in trouble, I look at the inputs needed to achieve the desired outcomes. If I see a learning challenge in a classroom or low numbers for a sales team, it's always a function of the input.

Choose your inputs wisely. Pressure to be competent in every area is bound to disappoint. Be strategic and timely with your efforts.

The Three Keys to Competency

1. Stay fresh.

Staying fresh requires intentional work. Just like an athlete must practice and train daily to be their best, we also can't expect results without doing the prep work and training. We have to consistently put fresh content in our minds. I know two major industry experts: one I still trust and the other not as much. One still delivers fresh content in each book and speech. The other is delivering the same content as years ago. This doesn't mean we have to be experts in multiple topics, but whatever our area, we have to keep

TRUST MATTERS

CLARITY

COMPASSION

CHARACTER

COMPETENCY

COMMITMENT

CONNECTION

CONTRIBUTION

CONSISTENCY

SOLVE WITH TRUST

current. Fresh perspectives, information, and experiences create an environment for innovation. It's crucial to success. What keeps you at prime condition for your role? You can't afford NOT to invest in it!

2. **Stay relevant.**

If you are a teacher who is teaching the same way you were 20 years ago, I probably won't trust you. If you are leading the same way you were 10 years ago or selling the exact same way you were five years ago, I probably won't trust you. People will only listen and follow your message if they can see why it matters now. Traveling, reading, and being part of a mastermind group can all help you stay relevant. For us, our annual study, the *Trust Outlook*®, is a way we spot trends and stay relevant to our audience.

3. **Stay capable.**

We not only have to build the muscle, but we also have to keep it. I know my horse can jump that log on the trail because she jumped a log twice that high last month. I know my event planner can handle all the details of a full-day training because she planned a two-day event with way more attendees earlier in the year. People like to know you've done *more* than they're asking you to do now. References from trusted sources build confidence in this way. You may be capable, but proof of it inspires trust like nothing else can.

Maintaining Competency After Success

Interestingly, the Competency Pillar can be most vulnerable on the heels of great success. When an organization loses the sense of urgency that fueled it in the early days, teams can find it difficult to stay motivated and hungry. Market leaders who have worked hard to build their business can sometimes fall into a "This is the way we've always done it" attitude that keeps them from learning and continuing to innovate. Beware of getting too comfortable with your current level of competency!

The Investment Will Pay Off

Employees become better and more resourceful performers when their place of work becomes a source of personal and professional enrichment. Along the way, individuals often become more engaged and committed to the company itself. When competency is high, trust increases, attrition goes down, and productivity goes up. *This* is how you invest in the future!

I will not forget the first time I witnessed the impact of training and development. Soon after I began this work, there was an organization that went all-in on our TELI research and work. First, we measured the organization's level of trust. Then, we trained *everyone* (not just the top leaders) in the 8-Pillar Framework. Here are the results:

- The whole organization enjoyed a common language.

- Engagement, performance, and trust scores rose significantly.

- Interactions from the hallways to the boardroom revealed a transformed culture.

- The COO told us they saved over $2 million in attrition costs within nine months.

It's the Training

Where competency is weak or compromised, there is typically complacency, arrogance, a lack of discipline, or too much reliance on the present routine. How can you systemize competency in your organization? Innovative organizations make staying fresh, relevant, and capable an ongoing priority.

In the fast-food world, the training separates the leader from the pack. Last year, the average revenue of both Taco Bell and Wendy's was around $1.9 million per store. Compare that with the behemoth McDonalds at $3.63 million per store annually. But who is number one by far at $6.71 million?[42] Hint, they work fewer hours than many franchises per day, *and* they take an entire day off per week. You might have guessed: Chick-fil-A.

It's not their chicken or even their sauce (really)! It's Chick-fil-A's training and development that builds competency and consistency in their employees. Chick-fil-A is by far the most efficient in getting people through their drive-through lines thanks to the way they equip and train their staff.[43] It's true that friendly employees are hired at other restaurants, but the staff at Chick-fil-A consistently treats customers kindly, ending with, "My pleasure." Do you think those 16-year-old cashiers were born saying, "My pleasure"? Absolutely not; they were trained! It's just one of the precision training methods Chick-fil-A uses to provide that warm, reliable experience that keeps customers coming back for more.

Building competency takes commitment and consistency, an excellent example of the pillars working together. When done right, you will see an uptick in everything from employee engagement and customer service to retention and bottom-line success.[44]

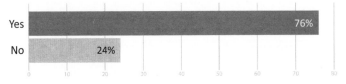

Would ongoing training help you trust your employer more?
Trust Outlook®

Yes — 76%
No — 24%

I knew Ritz-Carlton had an impeccable training program, so I asked the founder, Horst Schultze, what he did to create such a successful culture. Ritz-Carlton trains their employees on 12 values. *Isn't that way too many to remember and act on?* I wondered. He said it works because they train those values over and over. Every single day, before an employee starts their day of work, they go through a brief exercise based on the value of the day. Whether they are a manager or a housekeeper, everyone participates. It doesn't take long before people are familiar with all the values and maybe even feel a little bored. But the consistency pays off because after about six months, people buy in to the process. The values are internalized and naturally guide decision-making across the entire organization from top to bottom.

Building a Skills-First Culture

The job market is shifting quickly, and many workers can't keep up. The "skills gap" is so big that it's one of the main barriers preventing companies from modernizing their business model. Research by Deloitte confirms, "organizations building a skills-first culture are 63% more likely to achieve results."[45]

Critical Skills

According to the World Economic Forum, the following skills will be critical in the next five years:

- Creative thinking
- Analytical thinking
- Technological literacy
- Curiosity and lifelong learning
- Resilience, flexibility, and agility
- Systems thinking
- AI and big data
- Motivation and self-awareness
- Talent management
- Service orientation and customer service[46]

> ## The most important competency today is the desire and ability to learn fast.

COMPETENCY TRUST TOOLS

#16 **Input = Output**

#17 **Mentoring**

#18 **Feedback**

#19 **Mastermind Groups**

#20 **Cascading People Development Initiatives**

TRUST MATTERS

CLARITY

COMPASSION

CHARACTER

COMPETENCY

COMMITMENT

CONNECTION

CONTRIBUTION

CONSISTENCY

SOLVE WITH TRUST

Trust Tool #16: INPUT = OUTPUT™

Input affects output. What you put in determines what you get out.
Your life, your mind, your body, your community, and your work
culture all function this way. Don't allow yourself to get arrogant,
stagnant, or bored. Read something. Listen to something. Subscribe
to something. Do something!

INPUT   OUTPUT

The point of the Input = Output Trust Tool is to encourage you to
develop the habit of being a continual learner. I will provide you with
some ideas to get you started. Once your curiosity has been ignited,
you can create your own input plan that will work for you.

1. Read intentionally.

Reading brings a host of health benefits as well as increasing
intelligence, empathy, and even future wage-earning potential.

One study out of the University of Padua found that "those who read more books growing up ended up earning more money as an adult."[47] Bite-size options could be journals, white papers, or an online subscription in an area of interest.

According to the American Academy of Arts & Sciences, adult Americans read less than 16 minutes per day, as compared to watching nearly three hours of television. You'd think those with advanced degrees would read much more, but they reported reading an average of 28 minutes per day.[48] That means lots of people don't read at all. (Just for reading this book, you are officially above average!) After sharing these statistics at a conference, an older gentlemen wrote to me, "David, I was that guy who had not read a book since high school—if I even read one then! Since the conference, I started reading, and in the last 10 months, I have read 38 books. Your challenge *changed* me, even at my age! Thank you."

Readers not only become wise leaders, but they also tend to be innovative and humble. I've found that people who read regularly broaden their perspectives.

What are two topic areas where reading could broaden your current level of competency? How could you make it easy for yourself? Library? Audio books?

2. Listen to podcasts.

Podcasts are a great way to learn new things and gain new perspectives, all while driving your car or doing another daily activity.

❓ *When could you listen to a podcast during your daily routine? Which voices would expand your competency?*

3. Take classes or invest in formal education.

Advanced degrees can help advance careers. Over 20 years ago, I was on a weekend retreat and thought maybe I should get a higher degree in Organizational Leadership. I didn't have a good reason at the time. My work was going well. But that education launched me in ways I couldn't imagine at the time. It was the start of my trust research, consulting work, key relationships, books, and so much more. It is where I really found my passion and life calling. I am not saying that more formal education is for everyone, but I am grateful I took that step. Most learning institutions also have evening, online, or hybrid options to make their offerings accessible.

❓ *Is there an area where a class or a degree could level up your skills? Is there someone you could ask in your field who recently got a degree similar to what you would be interested in?*

4. Try a free online program or resource.

There is a plethora of online resources. From TED Talks to online courses, try searching for something that would both interest and benefit you.

❓ *What type of online course would you be curious about? Is there someone you know who could provide a recommendation for you?*

5. Hire a coach or seek out a mentor.

All accomplished individuals, from the greatest athletes to the most successful executives, have coaches and mentors who help them. Humility is the first step to ability. See Trust Tool #17: Mentoring for more.

> ❓ *Can you identify someone who could guide, coach, or mentor you? What is their area of specialty?*

6. Join a mastermind group.

Explore the leadership development groups available to you.For senior leaders, we offer TheTrustTable.com as a place where brilliant, diverse leaders sharpen each other. Most industries have associations you can join. Many local Chambers of Commerce also offer meetups where professionals across industries can share expertise. Or start your own! See Trust Tool #19: Mastermind Groups for more.

> ❓ *Is there a group you should consider being a part of? Do you know someone who could recommend one to you?*

7. Attend a conference or workshop.

Getting away or experiencing something new can spur innovation or further develop an idea you need in your profession. It can be a powerful experience to be surrounded by hundreds of others who are seeking knowledge on the same topic as you.

> ❓ *Is there an event you are interested in attending that could increase your competency? What financial, travel, and calendar adjustments would you need to plan for?*

8. Go somewhere new.

Traveling can increase our cultural competency, perspective, and people skills. Visit a new city or a new

TRUST MATTERS

CLARITY

COMPASSION

CHARACTER

COMPETENCY

COMMITMENT

CORRECTION

CONTRIBUTION

CONSISTENCY

SOLVE WITH TRUST

company in your industry. Bring donuts to a competitor or fellow leader across town and learn what it's like for them. I was just writing in my journal something I learned last week in a country halfway around the world from my home. We often gain fresh insight without even being aware of it when we travel or get out of our routine.

❓ *Is there a place nearby or far away that you've been hearing about? What strategic visit could you make to open your mind?*

Make an Input Plan

Set yourself up for success with a realistic timeframe; remember you can't be competent in everything, at least not all at once. The goal is to be constantly learning and build the habit of pursuing good inputs. If reading is part of your input plan, you might have a goal of 10 pages a day, a book a month, and 12 books a year. Or your plan could include simply listening to a podcast every time you exercise or drive to the office. Setting your learning goals in a realistic framework will give you motivation and provide pace to your overall strategy.

To get started, choose one to two input ideas to focus on. Choose a timeframe that makes sense according to your learning selection. Then write it down:

My Learning Plan

Input

Goal

Timeframe

This will be a good input because

My first step is

> *I have never accomplished anything great without the input of a mentor.* —DN

Trust Tool #17: MENTORING™

The concept of mentoring has been around since before Socrates mentored Plato who mentored Aristotle who mentored Alexander the Great who never lost in battle! Mentorship is perhaps the oldest and most potent form of training humanity has ever employed. From blacksmiths and carpenters to plumbers and tailors, many of our trade professions had (or still have) apprentices who eventually become the trusted experts.

TRUST MATTERS
CLARITY
COMPASSION
CHARACTER
COMPETENCY
COMMITMENT
CONNECTION
CONTRIBUTION
CONSISTENCY
SOLVE WITH TRUST

Merriam-Webster's Dictionary defines a mentor as "a trusted counselor or guide."[49] Others might describe a mentor as a wise, loyal, and supportive adviser or coach. Every accomplished person seems to credit the mentors who played a significant role in their life and career success. Mentors have certainly changed my life for the better.

Benefits of Having a Mentor

- The wisdom of greater experience

- A long-game perspective

- The gift of candid and constructive feedback

- A listening ear that will be honest and discreet

- Suggestions for growth from someone who knows you well

- Connections and opportunities with your best interest in mind

---

Mentoring is mutually beneficial to both people!

Finding a Mentor

1. Start by determining your main goal for having a mentor.

2. Identify role models according to those goals.

3. Reach out to one of them. Make it easy by just meeting once to explore the idea; leave room for them to say no without a big explanation or commitment.

4. Determine a regular time and place to meet that is convenient for them. Let them lead with how often to meet.

5. Always honor the gift they are giving you; respect their time and show appreciation.

Consider not just *what* you want to learn, but *who* you want to become. Brainstorm a list of people you look up to. Choose someone who seems to be doing and being what you would like to see for yourself in 10 years. Look for people who enjoy developing others, who love learning, and who are humble.

Are You a Mentor?

Perhaps you are in a place where *you* could mentor someone. Think about it. Consider the attributes that make a good mentor. Individuals who make time for mentoring frequently find the relationship to be just as encouraging and beneficial to them as it is for their mentee.

> *No matter your age or career stage, finding a mentor will impact your career. I use the Mentoring competency tool with my leadership development and executive coaching practice to connect experience with potential. Through the Mentoring tool, you will see increased confidence and capacity as well as improved teamwork and employee engagement.*
>
> —**Kellie Jo Kilberg**, President of Kilberg Consulting & Training

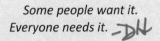

Trust Tool #18: FEEDBACK™

Where feedback is genuine, constructive, and from a trusted source, it remains the single most valuable way to learn. When we talk about feedback at TELI, we mean compassionate interactions built on top of strong connections in an environment where improving competency is normalized. Humility, curiosity, listening, and tactful communication are essentials for an environment that fosters healthy feedback.

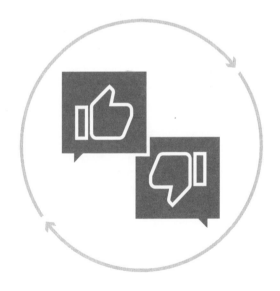

Giving Feedback

The backdrop for giving effective feedback is a trusted culture where compassion and connection are well established. Your employees and colleagues want to know where they stand with you, but *how* and *where* you share the feedback matters. If you are a manager of people, you know there is a long game and a short game to feedback, not to mention the many nuances to consider. This tool was designed to be a simple way for fast-moving leaders to engage constructively and keep improving.

Be consistent in giving feedback to all employees when you think it's appropriate. One of the most common findings from our institute's trust assessment, the Enterprise Trust Index™, is that people don't feel like there's fairness across an organization.

Avoid surprises in formal reviews; make sure you are giving and processing healthy feedback regularly. Don't save valuable feedback; it's often quicker and cleaner in the moment. Always have a discerning eye for time, place, privacy, and opportunity for response. If you use this tool frequently, your annual reviews should never last longer than an hour. Consider these steps for simple, ongoing feedback:

1. See it.

Watch for opportunities to praise as much as possible but don't shirk from sharing constructive feedback so people can grow. There is a fine line between being overly critical and being willing to have hard conversations. Think before you give unnecessary feedback. Ask yourself if it is kind and helpful.

2. Say it.

If it is positive, share it publicly. If it is constructive, share it privately. For the greatest impact, address it soon after you see it, so it is still fresh in everyone's mind. Consider how the individual receives feedback best. Be sensitive as well as specific, clear, and direct; use an example if appropriate.

3. Listen.

Be curious. Take feedback about your feedback. Do they have a different perspective that you didn't see at first? Do they have some thoughts that give clarity to the situation?

4. Move on.

Once you have shared and listened to a response, it is usually okay to move on, especially if healthy feedback is commonplace. Some people dwell on negative feedback too long. Once you have given it with clarity, give yourself permission to move on. If it needs to be addressed again, try Trust Tool #22: Six-Step Accountability Framework in the Commitment Pillar.

Receiving Feedback

The gift of feedback can make you and your organization better. Great leaders seek it from trusted sources. A *Harvard Business Review* article noted, "Real experts seek out constructive, even painful feedback. They're also skilled at understanding when and if a coach's advice doesn't work for them."[50] It's not enough to receive the feedback and thank the person for it. You need discernment to know what to *do* with the observations. Being honest with how to improve takes courage, time, and practice! While I encourage you to solicit feedback from clients, customers, vendors, and associates, this tool is about feedback between two colleagues.

Four Steps for Receiving Feedback

1. Ask for it genuinely. Specificity will be most helpful.

2. Thank those who gave it.

3. Process it for useful takeaways. This can be helpful to do with a trusted friend.

4. Act on it. Apply it as soon as you can or delete it instantly from your mind if it wasn't helpful.

Taking and applying feedback can be the fastest way to positive change.

TRUST MATTERS

CLARITY

COMPASSION

CHARACTER

COMPETENCY

COMMITMENT

CONNECTION

CONTRIBUTION

CONSISTENCY

SOLVE WITH TRUST

Trust Tool #19: MASTERMIND GROUP™

The most impactful learning often happens in a group setting. People have an amazing capacity to sharpen one another. Whether it's a taskforce of computer engineers, a group of senior leaders from different companies, a circle of HR managers, or a group of entrepreneurs that are all farmers, synergy can elevate a group to victory.

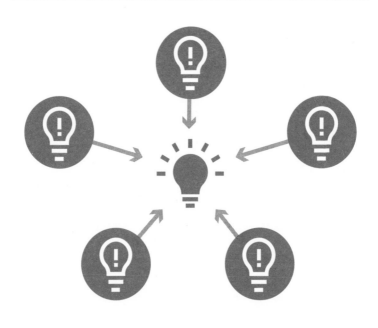

Mastermind Groups are typically made up of 5-15 people with relatively coequal roles who face similar challenges, hold each other accountable to personal and professional goals, and share best practices with each other on a regular basis. Leadership is shared or facilitated by a professional. Continuous learning becomes powerful when it is a team sport!

Benefits of a Mastermind Group

- Accountability

- Encouragement

- Fresh ideas, perspectives, and solutions

- Unseen opportunities

- Community networking

- Friendships

- Advice, challenge, and sharpening

- Solving problems faster

- Fulfillment

- Clarity in vision

- Greater success

When facing a roadblock, many minds are far more likely to uncover an answer than one. Belonging to a group can make you a more well-rounded person and can help you solve big issues more confidently. Sarah Kathleen Peck wrote in *Forbes*, "One of the key benefits of a mastermind is that it provides a space to unpack difficult puzzles and dig into the challenges you're working through."[51]

A Successful Mastermind Group

An effective Mastermind Group needs

☐ participants who can relate to each other on some level,

☐ a set of ground rules,

☐ a facilitator, unless members take turns,

☐ participants who are committed to attending,

☐ participants who are willing to be vulnerable and contribute,

☐ participants who want to learn,

☐ participants who are willing to listen,

☐ participants who have a bias toward generosity, and

☐ participants who are humble.

I'm part of a Mastermind Group made up of four guys. We've been meeting together for 30 years. We encourage each other and hold each other accountable for all sorts of things in our lives. I talk to at least one person from the group every week, and we all get together face-to-face at least once a year for several days to discuss each of our personal and professional goals and aspirations. Our connectedness and commitment to each other have been at times a rock and at other times a scalpel.

If you are feeling alone, get connected. Start now by making a list of potential members for a Mastermind Group you could initiate. Reach out. Even if you don't feel the need for support, you probably do, or you will someday. Visit TrustMattersBook.com/Mastermind to access some helpful accountability questions for mastermind groups.

TRUST MATTERS

CLARITY

COMPASSION

CHARACTER

COMPETENCY

COMMITMENT

CONNECTION

CONTRIBUTION

CONSISTENCY

SOLVE WITH TRUST

Stop burning your
training budget. ⌐DH

Trust Tool #20: CASCADING PEOPLE DEVELOPMENT INITIATIVES™

I have watched far too many organizations fail in their desperately needed people development initiatives. It doesn't have to be the case for you. If you're trying to cascade a people or leadership development initiative or program throughout your entire organization, then you need a comprehensive plan. The steps below incorporate the 8 Pillars of Trust to help you gain a common language and increase competency at scale.

Many times, leaders have great intentions, but they miss a crucial element. For example, losing a senior leader who is championing your organization's work on trust will cause progress to grind to a halt. We have seen the leaders in higher education, big tech, and the military leave or retire, and in each case, the culture improvements took a hit and previously successful development initiatives were discontinued.

> " Cascading trust must start at the highest level of an organization. One misaligned manager, department, or value will break the flow and lead to big challenges.
>
> —**Dave Cornell**, Author of *Cultivate Courage*, Speaker, Trainer, TELI Senior Consultant "

Effective Organizational Culture Change

Culture change can be daunting. This 10-step process breaks it down by pillar to help you see where and how to start. Using the combined strength of the pillars, vision is amplified, values are made relevant, a common language is built, and culture is strengthened.

If your culture is not what you want it to be, review these steps and see where you have gaps. Training and development initiatives have a chance of transforming cultures for the better when you follow and apply this 10-step tool.

1. **Stay aligned with your values and strategy.**
   (Clarity and Character Pillars)

   If a training initiative begins and your people quickly see *why* it matters to them right now, then they will buy in. If they see *how* it accelerates the company's current priorities and strategies, then they will buy in. Be clear with how this initiative fits in with what is already happening and advances everyone toward goal completion.

2. Find a senior leader champion.
(Commitment Pillar)

It's critical to have a champion. Someone needs to own it, lead it, and make sure everything aligns with it. Always be training new leaders so that if you lose your main champion, you can find a new one. Amplifying the strategic voices will increase buy-in. For one university transformation we were a part of, the main champion opened every training session with a video of himself explaining why the content that day aligned with the strategic initiatives of the university. Because of this, professors and staff joined together and got behind the program very quickly.

3. Teach it.
(Competency Pillar)

You need an intentional teaching plan if you want people to learn the new material, framework, or mindset. People want to learn and will often tell you what they need. Who can facilitate, educate, and coach them? Make a plan for the training sessions so they are never a waste. Include what you will do for those who miss the training. For important, culture-transforming work, everyone should get an initial training and after that, it should become part of the onboarding process to ensure everyone is on the same page.

4. Make it actionable today.
(Contribution Pillar)

If your people can see how the training will help them right away, it will give them hope, which builds momentum. If it's not actionable, it'll never get used. Make sure tools don't stay in theory. Make them usable and answer the relevancy question: What does this mean to us right now?

5. Provide a safe environment.
(Compassion Pillar)

If people don't feel safe, they don't learn. Take the time to think about how this training is going to come across differently to different segments of your group. Consider asking a few key individuals to give you feedback on the content, learning environment, culture, and teaching process to understand how to help it be effective for all people involved. Consider table size, discussion needs, departments together or separate, conversation time, and food sensitivities. Thinking through the implications of each element of the event will send the message that you care about creating a safe environment for all.

6. Include live interaction.
(Connection Pillar)

People want to be heard, and many internalize better when they verbally process. Live interaction is fun, makes points stick, and keeps everyone awake! Whether in-person or online, it also helps training ideas become customized and relevant. It's a good idea to make sure your facilitators are equipped and committed to guiding healthy interactions.

7. Measure change.
(Contribution Pillar)

If you don't measure it, it doesn't get prioritized or acted on. Get a baseline so you know where you are and have the ability to see progress. A quick pulse survey or small sample-interview process can ensure goals are getting accomplished. If the right training doesn't move the needle, something is wrong.

8. Provide healthy accountability.
(Commitment Pillar)

If there aren't rewards or ramifications tied to the work, people won't be motivated to make it a priority. Training results can be revisited and evaluated more easily than you think. Consider incorporating accountability into your measurement process. When people are held accountable and there is a consequence for lack of productivity or performance, it puts more weight on the agreed-upon priorities and encourages alignment.

9. Reinforce consistently.
(Consistency Pillar)

Without reinforcement, we forget. The only way to create a common language is through consistency. Don't start training if there is no plan for reinforcement. One way we have seen consistency take hold is by inviting a small group of culture ambassadors to meet every month to answer, "How are we keeping this common language and set of tools thriving here?"

Consistent reinforcement of language and content are the tracks for the rest of the trust train to run on. Just like the famous children's book, *The Little Engine That Could*, "I think I can, I think I can, I think I can" signifies the consistent effort required to succeed.[52] One-and-done initiatives or flavor-of-the-month trainings and assessments usually fail. It's best to create a simple, consistent system of ongoing reinforcement.

10. Help the organization AND individuals.
(Compassion Pillar)

If your leadership and people development initiatives only help the organization and don't help the person get better, it won't stick. Organizations don't change. Only people do. That's why application must be personal first.

> When competency is high,
> trust increases, attrition goes down,
> and productivity goes up.

Increasing competency is an investment in *your* future.

Dedication matters.

Pillar 5: Commitment

People believe in those who stand through adversity.

THINK ABOUT ANYONE who has left a lasting legacy in your life or in the world. Your first grade teacher, your parents, Nelson Mandela, Martin Luther King Jr., Mother Theresa, Ghandi, Joan of Arc, or Jesus Christ—they all had something in common. They were committed to something beyond themselves. All of them were willing to stay on mission in the face of adversity, in some cases to their death. These examples of caring beyond self, remaining steadfast in the face of adversity, and uniting others to support their causes dramatically influenced the world.

Commitment is living by convictions not comfort. Commitment yields devotion, loyalty, and followership.

TRUST MATTERS

CLARITY

COMPASSION

CHARACTER

COMPETENCY

COMMITMENT

CONNECTION

CONTRIBUTION

CONSISTENCY

SOLVE WITH TRUST

Why Commitment Matters

- *Commitment weathers adversity.* Challenges are certain. Only those who are dedicated in the midst of the storm make it through.

- *Keeping commitments is the only way to rebuild trust.* People often think trust is rebuilt on an apology, but it is only restored when a promise is kept.

- *Dedication is the path to accomplishing goals and exceeding outcomes.* Nothing great happens without committed people.

- *Without commitment, you won't have followers.* Commitment is seldom reciprocated if people don't feel the leader is committed to them.

- *Big sacrifices equal big results.* If you ever see an amazing outcome, it's the result of someone's sacrifice of time, energy, or both.

Commitment Will Help You Stand Apart

Commitment at work used to mean clocking in and out (on time) for 30 or 40 years. Now, there is fading loyalty between employees and employers. Pro-athletes are less committed to their teams, and teams are less committed to them. Commitment to our country, our ideals, and our institutions has fallen. It is easier than ever to exit commitments and relationships. Are we just selfish or lazy? Have we elevated our feelings above our virtues? Or perhaps we've simply experienced too many breaches of trust. Whatever the reason, making and keeping commitments stands out today.

A person who can be relied on to stick to their commitments brings great benefit to the productivity of any workplace. Employees who don't have personal or professional commitments tend to be disengaged from their job and often from life in general. These disengaged employees cost the world an estimated $8.8 trillion in lost productivity: that's equal to 9% of the global GDP![53] Imagine what we could accomplish if more of us would allow ourselves to fully commit.

It's the Little Things

Commitment is demonstrated in the little daily actions we repeat. In *Atomic Habits,* James Clear noted, "Every action you take is a vote for the type of person you wish to become."[54] Life isn't about huge transformations as much as it's about establishing a framework that supports small steps toward success. It's about making and keeping commitments, treating people with compassion, and demonstrating good character—all the things we've been talking about in the 8 Pillars of Trust. Getting back to someone. Being on time. Getting up to the first sound of the alarm. When you make and keep these little daily commitments, you build trust in yourself. Those who don't trust themselves have a hard time building it with others.

Commitment Weathers Adversity

It's easy to be a positive and kind leader when you are thriving, but when you experience headwinds, that's when commitment shows its depth. I think of the thousands of leaders who stood strong and weathered the storms of the COVID-19 pandemic. I watched leaders win and lose during that trying time; some lost in spite of their efforts. This large-scale impact gave us a chance to see what really mattered to people. Those who survived the adversity showed unwavering commitment.

When you are committed to a task or to a relationship, you've given a promise to follow through on your choice. There is freedom in not wondering what you should do when troubles come; you've already decided. Clear commitment helps you maintain a sense of purpose and provides a direction for action.

When my wife and I decided to start a business together in 1999, we were planning to secure some side jobs to make ends meet. We were living in a musty basement with black mold and no windows, and we were down to $1.40 after paying our urgent bills. My brother advised us to stay focused on the goal, and he believed that if we did, we would succeed. Lisa and I stayed committed to our goal of starting a new business without side gigs. There were some rough moments, but his advice worked for us.

People believe in those who stand through adversity.

Commitment Must Be Earned

Do you wish people would be more committed to you or more committed to the company? Many people have tried to produce, require, or even demand commitment. I'll never forget a time when I was asked to share an opening keynote address with several thousand salespeople at a company's global sales kickoff. The new Senior Vice President of Sales opened the meeting before he introduced me. He told his people they should be committed to *him* and to "just trust *him*." He lost his team that day.

Trust and commitment are not won through words; they are earned. The best way to nurture commitment from your team is to go out of your way to demonstrate it yourself.

People can sense genuineness from miles away.

Far too many times, I have watched leaders fail to keep commitments because they did not count the cost, or they flippantly lived for a moment of admiration from their people. If you are inauthentic, it will sabotage commit from others. Be as transparent as you can be. Reveal your determination and intent. You don't receive commitment without showing it.

Personal Accountability

Making and keeping commitments to yourself builds capacity to follow through in other areas of your life. Promise-keeping leaders tend to invite accountability.

The American Society of Training and Development's study on accountability predicts the probability of completing a goal:

- If you *have* an idea or a goal – 10%

- If you *consciously decide* you will do it – 25%

- If you decide *when* you will do it – 40%

- If you *plan how* you will do it – 50%

- If you *commit to someone* you will do it – 65%

- If you have a *specific accountability appointment* with a person you've committed to – 95%[55]

TRUST MATTERS

CLARITY

COMPASSION

CHARACTER

COMPETENCY

COMMITMENT

CONNECTION

CONTRIBUTION

CONSISTENCY

SOLVE WITH TRUST

PROBABILITY OF COMPLETING A GOAL

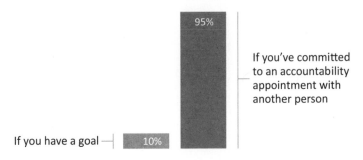

If you've committed to an accountability appointment with another person — 95%

If you have a goal — 10%

Partner up with someone or invite a mentor or trusted colleague to ask you the hard questions. Exercise accountability to keep your commitments; it will inspire others to do the same!

> People are 9x more likely
> to complete a goal if they've
> committed to accountability.

Loyalty at Work

We've talked about personal and professional commitments and inviting accountability, but what about commitment to a specific job or organization? According to the World Economic Forum, loyalty in the business world has been declining for the better part of two decades. Their survey indicated that only half of employees are satisfied with their jobs. Think about it: the average millennial worker is now about 40 years old and in the prime of their career.[56] This generation has seen their parents lose promised pensions and jobs just before retirement. They have rarely experienced loyalty from their employer, at least not to the degree that earlier generations did, so why would leaders and managers expect them to show loyalty in return? With a culture that is more accepting of leaving contracts and relationships, we definitely have a commitment problem.

If we establish greater commitment in both directions (employee to company and company to employee), then in times of crisis, employees are much more likely to rally together, demonstrate flexibility, and contribute to creative solutions rather than abandoning ship.

We asked American workers, "What percentage of your career have you had a leader or employer you could fully trust?" About half of workers said "little" of their work life has been spent with a leader or employer they could fully trust. It's hard to be committed to someone you don't trust.

What percentage of your career have you had a leader/employer you could fully trust?

Trust Outlook®

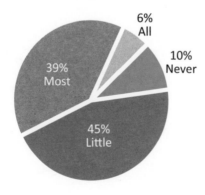

6%
All

10%
Never

39%
Most

45%
Little

Trusted leaders take responsibility for mistakes and follow
through to make sure there is resolution. They avoid deflecting
blame onto others, apologize quickly, and make a commitment to
stay with it until there is a full remedy to the situation. People will
not follow a leader they do not trust.

The Joy of Sacrifice

A large population of our society has grown fixated on individualism
which tends to put self before others. Brad Stulberg, author of *The
Practice of Groundedness*, said, "Heroic individualism says that you
will never have enough, be enough, or do enough. It is an endless
gauntlet of more, more, more,"[57] and it's making people lose sight
of what it means to sacrifice as a team. People are investing less and
less emotional energy into their jobs and volunteerism. Sadly, this
means they are missing out on the joy of service and sacrifice, not to
mention the confidence that is built when someone generously gives
of themselves.

We can be part of significant change if we model healthy
sacrifice to achieve something great with a team of people. The
feeling of belonging to a committed team beats any financial
"employee benefit."

The Combined Strength of the Pillars

We are deep into the 8 Pillars of Trust, and I hope you can start
to see how they are interdependent. For example, Clarity plus
Commitment equals commitments that last. Also, expecting
Competency is good, but even better when done with Compassion.
Watch for the interconnected pillars in this amazing story about
rebuilding trust in Rwanda.

TRUST MATTERS

CLARITY

COMPASSION

CHARACTER

COMPETENCY

COMMITMENT

CONNECTION

CONTRIBUTION

CONSISTENCY

SOLVE WITH TRUST

Committed to Rebuilding Trust:
The Greatest Example in 100 Years

Rwanda, a place and people I have come to love, is home to one of the most horrific genocides in history. The tragic history of Rwanda goes back to colonial times, where the divisions in their society were perpetuated over time by the elite. This erosion in trust led to the massacres of Tutsis in the 60s and 70s and culminated in the infamous genocide of 1994. Over the course of 100 days, as the world stood by, over one million Tutsis were killed, property was destroyed, neighbors turned on each other, and over two million Rwandans became refugees.[58]

I've heard my Rwandan friends giving testimonies of this horrific time in their history: One friend watched his family be murdered while he hid safely behind a cupboard door. Another, Ambassador Mathilde Mukantabana, was miraculously spared because she was out of the country when nearly every member of her family was killed.

The oppressive regime was finally overthrown by a national group which stopped the bloodshed. Today, Rwanda continues to recover, thanks to the intentional efforts and commitments of Rwandan citizens and leaders.

Here is a partial list of the actions that the people of Rwanda took and continue to undertake to rebuild trust:

1. Strict laws have been created to **prevent people from sowing similar seeds of hatred** that led to disastrous divisions. They also established the Gacaca Courts, which are community tribunals designed to try perpetrators, promote justice at the local level, and facilitate reconciliation.

2. Rwanda has started **educational programs promoting values of tolerance, unity, and forgiveness,** especially for young people who need to learn their country's history. The government emphasizes the importance of a shared national identity above ethnic divides via their "I am Rwandan" campaign. Most people no longer self-identify as Hutus or Tutsi, but collectively as Rwandan.

3. Rwandan leadership has encouraged several grassroots organizations to **support peacebuilding and economic development programs** at the community level. Healing teams were established and traveled the country with messages and invitations for both survivors and perpetrators—giving both the opportunity to advance forgiveness and reconciliation. The Ministry of National Unity and Reconciliation promotes social cohesion and a safe space for dialogue between different groups. The Rwandan government even established a Reconciliation Barometer to measure and inspire progress.

4. Rwanda is making significant strides toward **building an inclusive economy** that leaves no one behind by teaching entrepreneurship and employment readiness to youth. Take their Girinka program for example. One cow per family gives those living in the rural areas a tremendous boost in life.

While there is more yet to be done, Rwanda has achieved unprecedented economic growth, a declining poverty rate, and a 20-year increase in life expectancy from 49 years in 2000 to 69.6 years in 2022![59] Rwanda is now known for being a peace-building country and is one of the safest countries in the world.[60] What a turnaround in just 30 years! Rwanda's remarkable progress shows us what is possible if we focus on building trust.[61]

COMMITMENT TRUST TOOLS

#21 **Personal Commitment Reflection**

#22 **Six-Step Accountability Framework**

#23 **10 Steps to Rebuild Trust**

TRUST MATTERS
CLARITY
COMPASSION
CHARACTER
COMPETENCY
COMMITMENT
CONNECTION
CONTRIBUTION
CONSISTENCY
SOLVE WITH TRUST

Trust Tool #21:
PERSONAL COMMITMENT REFLECTION™

Have you ever had someone make a commitment to you but not keep it? Pretty frustrating, isn't it? What about you? Have you ever made a commitment that you have not kept? We often judge ourselves by our intentions and others by their actions. Here is your opportunity to examine your commitments. Trusted leaders choose their commitments carefully and evaluate themselves often.

VALUES   PROMISES   DANGERS

To apply this tool, you will need

- about 20 minutes of quiet time,
- a copy of your Personal Mission Statement or Decision-Making Values to review,

- your calendar,
- a place to journal (paper or digital notebook), and
- the questions below.

Start by reflecting on your Mission, Values, and Priorities (Trust Tool #6) or Personal Mission Statement (Trust Tool #14). Then open your calendar and look over the last few weeks. Go through the questions below and record or journal your answers. Avoid yes or no answers. Input equals output on this exercise.

Reflection Questions

Values
☐ Does my time with my family reflect my values?

☐ Does my time with my friends reflect my values?

☐ Does my time with my coworkers reflect my values?

Promises
☐ Am I making promises to my family I'm not keeping?

☐ Am I making promises to my friends I'm not keeping?

☐ Am I making promises to my coworkers I'm not keeping?

Dangers
☐ Am I in danger of losing trust with my family by not fulfilling commitments?

☐ Am I in danger of losing trust with my friends by not fulfilling commitments?

☐ Am I in danger of losing trust with my coworkers by not fulfilling commitments?

Look back over your answers and circle or highlight one to two areas of conviction to work on. Reflect on any underlying root beliefs or habits that are causing the overcommitment or lack of follow-through. Identify one action you can take to move the needle in the next week. Don't choose something unless you are willing to address it. Write down your action item and put it somewhere you will see it every day.

For the best return on your investment, we recommend revisiting this tool quarterly. More often is helpful if you are trying to solidify stronger commitments. It is also a great check-up tool if you're feeling like your commitments have slipped over time.

If you start noticing a chronic pattern, it may be appropriate to ask a mentor or supportive colleague for accountability.

TRUST MATTERS

CLARITY

COMPASSION

CHARACTER

COMPETENCY

COMMITMENT

> *Use this tool to align what is said with what is done.* ✒DH

Trust Tool #22: SIX-STEP ACCOUNTABILITY FRAMEWORK™

I often see two extremes in the workplace that lead to unhealthy accountability: 1) poisonous micromanagement or 2) avoiding holding people accountable altogether. Being over-bearing *or* apathetic leads to disengagement. Healthy account-ability takes work, wisdom, and discernment and is a must for high-trust cultures. Domineering accountability can lead to people feeling micromanaged; avoiding accountability can lead to people losing confidence.

GOAL?

ABILITY?

SUCCESS?

CHECK-IN?

RESULTS?

OWNERSHIP?

I'll never forget working with a leader who had eight reports. Seven were good and one was lazy. The lazy report came in late and provided shoddy work at best. Who was everyone frustrated with? Not the lazy guy as much as you might think. The team started to be bitter toward the leader because he was avoiding the work of healthy accountability.

Responsibility Versus Accountability

What is the difference between *responsibility* and *accountability*? I define responsibility as something I can hold *myself* to. As in, "I can hold myself responsible for getting that done." Whereas accountability is something I can hold *others* to. As a leader, I can hold others accountable, or they can hold me accountable. Therefore, it is much easier to have an accountable culture if you first hire responsible people! No matter how much personal responsibility one shows, a leader's job is to hold others accountable in a healthy way.

Accountability is a metric with a recurring conversation that has clear ramifications for performance. It is an openly shared goal to align what is said with what is done. It works best when people know they are valued, decisions are driven down close to the point of impact, and individuals desire to be responsible. Ideally, accountability is invited, but even if you embrace the process, it doesn't mean it will be easy!

Accountability Questions

This tool is for supervisors, managers, or coaches who want to take the guess work out of managing a person or a team. Before you start, remember, the Compassion Pillar comes before the

Commitment Pillar intentionally. People will have a hard time being accountable to someone they don't believe cares about them. In order for this tool to be effective, you need to show compassion and establish genuine connection first.

The Six-Step Accountability Framework provides questions to clarify commitments when you are in a one-on-one conversation with someone who needs or is inviting accountability.

1. Clear Goal

Am I clear about the goal? Is it a shared goal? Take time to make sure you're aligned with leadership and with overall priorities. Be specific with a due date.

2. Clear Ability

Do I have the personal capability and needed resources to follow through on my commitment? Time spent here will eliminate conflict and frustration later on. It is hard to hold someone accountable to a task if they were never given access to the right resources.

3. Clear Metric

What does success look like? What measures would indicate progress? Does this need daily or weekly attention? Having metrics along the way allows for appropriate evaluation and the ability to pivot when it makes sense.

4. Clear Check-in

How are we staying connected and informed as we pursue our goal? Decide ahead of time how you will track progress and communicate. How often will you reassess?

5. Clear Results

What are the rewards for success or the repercussions for failure? Rewards and consequences should be connected to results and decided ahead of time. Make sure they know how they can WIN.

6. Clear Commitment

What percentage of this will I own? To get a pulse on how committed someone is, I sometimes ask, "1-10, how committed are you to this goal and timeline?" If we have a solid relationship, I get an insightful answer.

Answer the questions together with the person (or team) you are holding accountable. As a leader, predetermine any boundaries you need to give or answers you'd like to direct them to. You can visit TrustMattersBook.com/Accountability to access a helpful accountability reference card.

Commitment may be
expressed in words, but
it is demonstrated through
consistent action.

Possible Reponses

If you're a leader responding to the success or failure of a goal, it helps to decide ahead of time what your options or next steps will be. Here are four ways to consider responding, following a period of accountability:

1. Redo

Give the person or team another chance to address, resolve, improve, or meet the goal.

2. Reward

Celebrate success through public acknowledgment, time off, or a small gift.

3. Repercussion

Consequences must be established and followed up on in order to create an accountable, high-trust culture. Pre-decide what is appropriate.

4. Release

If a person is not a good fit for this project or role, action must be taken to remove or reassign them for the benefit of all.

> *Everyone will have to rebuild trust.*
> *Here's how.* ‑DN

Trust Tool #23:
10 STEPS TO REBUILD TRUST™

What happens when you need to rebuild trust? Did you fail some-one? Did your personal or corporate reputation take a hit? What if your brand no longer carries any weight? There's no easy way around it. You have to work to get it back.

All the principles we use to build trust in the first place also apply in rebuilding trust. Think of specific ways to apply each Pillar of Trust to the relationship you're repairing.

Rebuilding a Personal Breach of Trust

1. Acknowledge the breach and what led to it.

2. Apologize sincerely to the people affected by your mistake.

3. Move quickly to take personal responsibility. Don't be afraid to acknowledge more than your share; it usually reciprocates.

4. Empathetically listen. Repeat back what you're hearing for added clarity.

5. Make actionable plans to do better: consider which of the pillars are most weak at this time and use the How? How? How? Trust Tool to define an action you can take today to begin solving the problem.

6. Commit to and follow through on repairing the relationship. In what ways could you connect with this person that would mean the most to them and demonstrate that you heard them?

7. Consider if there needs to be a shift in responsibility to eliminate all or a part of the issue that led to the breach. Perhaps it's just for a time or you agree to accountability from an outside party.

8. Communicate often during a time of rebuilding.

9. Consider starting over in some meaningful way or redefining boundaries and expectations.

10. Make and keep a commitment. Repeat.

Rebuilding a Corporate Breach of Trust

1. Acknowledge the issues surrounding the breach.

2. Apologize sincerely: this may need to be in public and in several formats.

3. Move quickly to take responsibility. As a leader, it's usually better to own a corporate mistake even if it's not all your fault. Someone must voice the apology and show remorse; do it authentically for the good of all.

4. Empathetically listen to all. Record listening sessions, take surveys, start a website or blog to walk the community through updates.

5. Make actionable plans to do better. Consider which of the pillars are most weak at this time and use the How? How? How? Trust Tool to define an action you can take today to begin solving the problem. You will need to consider specific plans for different agencies or departments depending on how they were affected.

6. Commit to and follow through on repairing the relationships. Consider the network of damage and be strategic with who repairs relationships with whom. Consider some targeted social events to allow people to let off steam in a healthy way. Find creative ways to connect with those affected the most.

7. Consider a leadership change especially in the event of an ethical breach, but also if certain leaders lack the capabilities needed for future success.

8. Clarify and share a new vision. Create a long-term communication plan. Expect to overcommunicate.

9. Be willing to take public accountability and show more transparency until trust is rebuilt. Consider cutting ties or rebranding to separate yourself from something if you have genuinely resolved the core issue.

10. Make and keep a commitment. Repeat.

The only way to rebuild trust is to *make and keep* a new commitment.

Tips

- **Don't expect a quick return of trust.** Even if you're forgiven or it wasn't your fault, rebuilding trust takes longer than breaking it.

- **People appreciate the apology but trust the follow-through.** A commitment becomes more powerful when you declare it publicly and invite open accountability. Don't make the commitment lightly because your lack of keeping it will lose even more trust if it's public.

TRUST MATTERS

CLARITY

COMPASSION

CHARACTER

COMPETENCY

COMMITMENT

CONNECTION

CONTRIBUTION

CONSISTENCY

SOLVE WITH TRUST

Collaboration matters.

Pillar 6:
Connection

*People want to follow, buy from, and be around
those who connect and collaborate.*

TRUST CANNOT EXIST without connection, and connection
cannot exist without trust. People need each other. In *The
Genius Myth*, Michael Meade argues that nothing great has ever
been done alone. Who invented the light bulb? Thomas Edison,
right? Even though he often gets the full credit, there were a
number of scientists on his team, not to mention other scientists
around the world also working at the same time on making the
light bulb work better and last longer.[62] What about the cotton
gin in 1794? We learned in school it was Eli Whitney, but plantation owner Catherine Green, plantation manager Phineas Miller,
and many of those enslaved on the Mulberry Grove plantation
likely played a big role in the invention.[63] If you look back at
history, every invention credited to one person really stands
for multiple people making that innovation come to fruition.
Nothing of significance has ever been done alone.

Books are a great example. I'm the author, but researchers from our institute, editors, the publisher, the graphic designer, advance-copy readers, and my family all had a significant hand in it coming to reality...yet my name is on the cover. The bigger the problem or challenge, the greater the need for a strong Connection Pillar.

Why Connection Matters

- ***Humans have an innate need to belong.*** They crave it. They need it. They seek ways to fulfill this need from birth to death.

- ***Connected people live longer.*** Studies have shown that connecting with others is literally good for your health.[64]

- ***Trust cannot be maintained without connection.*** It's impossible to connect in relationships that have little or no trust.

- ***Connected employees STAY.*** Just as in any school, club sport, fitness center, church, public library, store, or business where people feel connected, they will gather, join, come back to, and feel a sense of belonging.

- ***Nothing of significance has ever been done alone***. Whether it be a supportive friend or a huge team of engineers, nothing great is ever done by just one person.

- ***Connection is the FASTEST way to build trust.*** Trust can be built slowly over time, but in the presence of a strong connection such as a common vision, shared values, similar experiences, or common friends and colleagues, trust can be built more quickly.

Connection Requires Intentionality

It used to be commonplace that a neighbor or friend would knock on the door because they wanted to chat with you. Now we get startled when the doorbell rings unexpectedly! We are hardwired to value interpersonal connection and experiences, yet our expectations regarding privacy and community have changed.

With so many electronic communication methods available, leaders of today need to be innovative and intentional about connecting with their people.

People Need to Know and Be Known

In her TED Talk, author and development psychologist Susan Pinker describes the commonality of the places where people live the longest. There is only one place in the world where the men have an equal life expectancy to women, and there is a higher-than-average size population of centenarians (people over 100 years old). This community of people live in what is referred to as a "Blue Zone" on the small Italian island of Sardinia. The residents of this Mediterranean island don't eat special food or have particularly amazing genetics. They live in small houses and are close to their neighbors and family which invites and even forces consistent connections. According to Pinker, they are socially integrated. *They are not lonely.* They have daily small interactions and conversations with everyone they meet. This "forms a biological force field against disease and decline."[65] The real secret to a healthy personal and professional life is connection.

TRUST MATTERS

CLARITY

COMPASSION

CHARACTER

COMPETENCY

COMMITMENT

CONNECTION

CONTRIBUTION

CONSISTENCY

SOLVE WITH TRUST

Lululemon, Starbucks, and Harley Davidson are examples of companies who understand the power of connection. Lululemon, the high-end active clothing company, has created brand awareness and loyalty by providing free events in their communities. They offer free yoga classes and monthly talks at their local stores. They have a global reach that has been built by connecting in ways that make their customers feel part of the community. One of Lululemon's slogans is: *Think global, act local.*[66]

One of the police departments that is using our TELI material said they noticed a significant difference compared to nearby communities in their ability to mitigate and calm racial tension. As a department, they have embraced the 8 Pillars of Trust. In doing so, they've connected black and white officers and citizens through listening sessions, joint community activities, and intentional stops to play basketball around town with young people. It has all worked together to raise the level of trust the community feels in their police department. The Police Chief in this city said, "Our work with TELI helped us plant the seeds of trust with our community. These connecting and trust-building efforts have kept our community from having the social and racial tensions many others have experienced. Even during this difficult time for policing, we are experiencing support and care."

Connection in the Workplace

Connections are essential for everyone to feel a sense of belonging. When connection is loose or compromised, cliques, isolation, organizational silos, or individualism creeps in. A weak connection exaggerates *every* problem. Sarah Laoyan says, "Silos can be negatively reinforced through turf wars, unclear vision, and a lack of communication. This can lead to decreased interactions with necessary teams, duplicative work, and resistance to change."[67] She goes on to share that some organizations even incentivize a lack of connection by forcing teams to "use up their budget or not get it next year whether they need it or not." This motivates siloing which keeps people from using resources for the greater good of the whole.

Fostering a greater sense of connection in teams increases speed and accuracy of communication, strengthens resilience, and reduces stress. When people feel a sense of connection and belonging at work, they are willing to share information, they engage, they are productive, and they stay.

Friends in the Workplace

Recent Gallup data found that having a best friend at work increases engagement, business outcomes, innovation, profitability, and retention. These employees are more likely to get more done in less time *and* have fun while at work. Social connection is important, but even more important is having someone you can rely on during a difficult stretch in life or at work.[68] Unfortunately, a survey by BetterUp in 2022 revealed these results:

- Percentage of people who don't look forward to working because of coworkers – 53%

- Percentage of people who don't feel a sense of connection to coworkers – 43%

- Percentage of people who don't trust their coworkers – 38%

- Percentage of people who don't have even one friend at work – 22%[69]

TRUST MATTERS

CLARITY

COMPASSION

CHARACTER

COMPETENCY

COMMITMENT

CONNECTION

CONTRIBUTION

CONSISTENCY

SOLVE WITH TRUST

Friendships can't be forced, but they can be encouraged. Leaders play a key role in fostering an environment where authentic connection has space to form organically. At its core, trust is about relationships. In a hybrid or remote work environment where physical distance can easily translate into emotional distance, fostering genuine connections is not only challenging but it is also critical. Here's what we learned about people's preference for working remote or in person and in what environment they can more easily build trust:

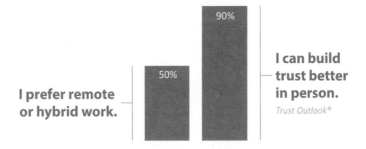

I prefer remote or hybrid work. 50%

I can build trust better in person. 90%
Trust Outlook®

Benefits of Authentic Engagement

I frequently meet business leaders who say, "I'd really like to increase employee engagement." The problem is you don't get engagement with more engagement. You need to increase trust; that's what leads to more engagement.

> People trust those who are
> willing to connect.

One CEO, after administering our Enterprise Trust Index™ (ETI) to his teams, was able to identify two key gaps across a large dealership organization. First, he found an opportunity to increase trust between executive leadership and the front-line employees. Then once every quarter, he visited regional offices for lunch. While not considered a polished speaker, he made the effort to share a 10-minute update before lunch. After every update, he thanked the employees he was sitting with, took time to connect current strategy to the mission and vision, and made a few minutes available for questions. He also reinstituted one-on-one meetings, so everyone had a predictable and consistent meeting with their manager. This company's Trust Score rose massively by the time they took their next ETI.

Alone at the Top

Walking the journey with a few influential leaders who are alone at the top has been a significant and rewarding part of my work over the last decade. There is a part of leadership that necessitates individual responsiblity. Leaders often carry a weight that only they can carry. Leaders can't share everything; they have to be discerning. Some information isn't fair, kind, or even legal to share with others.

Leaders often need to find connections outside their work-place. Every leader needs a small group of confidantes they can count on for encouragement, wisdom, and accountability. When I think of any success I have enjoyed, it is because of close, transparent relationships with people who both had my back and were willing to get in my face.

Connect Through Honesty

People frequently wish to hide their mistakes and failings out of the belief that if they reveal those parts of themselves, others will respect them less. In actuality, the opposite is often true. The more open and honest you are about your mistakes, the more people are willing to trust you, protect you, and give you the benefit of the doubt. We might admire someone's strengths, but we connect on their shortcomings. When was the last time you told someone a story of a time you failed?

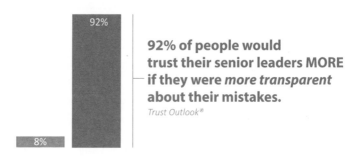

92% of people would trust their senior leaders MORE if they were *more transparent* about their mistakes.
Trust Outlook®

Board Room Vulnerability

I once stood at the front of a conference room while the leadership team of a tech start-up company started to fill the meeting room. I was brought in to help. There was energy in the room but not of the best kind. It was nervous energy. The company was burning through cash and failing to make deadlines. I lost track of how many people came up to me before the meeting and started to say something like, "We will deliver on this next product deadline. We have to or else we are done." "Thanks for being here. We got this." I started to get the feeling the team was just saying these things to convince themselves that it wasn't that bad. It was made clear that they needed to deliver or else the last investors would likely pull their funding.

I started the meeting by saying, "I know you must make this next deadline, but just to get a feel, on a scale of 1 to 10 with 10 being certain, how certain are you that you will deliver it on time?" Many people chimed in around the same time. I heard, "9, 10, 9, 8." Then one of the more junior members of the team chimed in with a low-pitched tone: "3." Her words rang hollow, and in that moment, the oxygen was sucked out of the room.

Everyone knew it was true.

Fear and worry covered the faces of some. For others, there was a look of relief that someone had the guts to tell the truth. Because this young leader was courageous enough to be vulnerable, we were able to deal with the big issue immediately that day. I'm happy to say that they met their deadline, and the company was saved, but it never would have happened if we had waited to discuss the truth and the reasons why they were missing their deadlines. Safe environments that foster trust and encourage healthy vulnerability can enrich relationships and save companies. It did that day.

Diversity at Its Best

People won't connect if they don't feel safe. In the *Trust Outlook*®, we found a range of conflicting views about diversity. People say they believe diversity is important for high-performing teams, yet most people say they prefer to work on teams with people just like themselves. We know we can gain enormous advantages from a renewed focus on diversity, equity, and inclusion *but only if the diversity is paired with TRUST.*

Is diversity important for a
high-performing team?
Trust Outlook®

| 89% | Diversity *is* important. |

| 11% | Diversity is *not* important. |

Harvard political scientist Robert Putnam's well-known research on diversity was based on detailed phone calls with 30,000 Americans. Putnam concluded that "In the most diverse communities, neighbors trust one another about half as much as they do in the most homogenous settings."[70] We know diversity spurs creativity and innovation, AND we also know people like to have something in common.

Who do you want to work alongside?
Trust Outlook®

| 24% | People who are a lot *different* than you. |

| 76% | People who are a lot *like* you. |

How do we leverage the best of diversity? Invite diversity of race, backgrounds, and perspectives for creativity, innovation, and the ability to serve all people well, but guard against diversity of values, vision, or mission—or you will lose your culture, identity, and common language.

Diversity of Perspectives + **Sameness** of Values / Mission = **BEAUTIFUL OUTCOMES**

Value Diversity + Build Connection

1. *Be curious.* A quick process for insightful questions is Trust Tool #25: Curious Questions.

2. *Be crystal clear* about your vision and values.

3. *Incentivize cultural intelligence* through training, coaching, time, and consistent communication. David Livermore's book, *Leading with Cultural Intelligence* and accompanying assessment significantly helped a board on which I serve grow in capacity.[71]

4. *Identify the combinations of skill sets and strengths* that connect for the best outcomes in your field. Celebrate them and train your teams to collaborate and utilize those skills.

Collaboration Matters

Teams are a key driver of success in nearly every sector of business. Whether it's the Formula 1 pit crew, the world-famous Mayo Clinic, or the civil engineers working on a new skyscraper, collaboration and connection is required!

CONNECTION TRUST TOOLS

#24 **Magnetic vs.
Repelling Traits**

#25 **Curious Questions**

#26 **Storytelling**

#27 **Engagement Statement**

#28 **The Solving Circle**

#29 **Five Ways to Build Virtual Trust**

> *Be the one who lights up the room!* ~DH

Trust Tool #24:
MAGNETIC VS. REPELLING TRAITS™

There are magnetic personality traits we all want to see more of, and there are repelling traits we all want to see less of. Arrogance and self-importance push people away, while expressing appreciation and gratitude draws people in. One might assume the ability to light up a room is innate and exclusive to those who are outgoing and charismatic, but there are much deeper traits that can be cultivated that will make any personality shine!

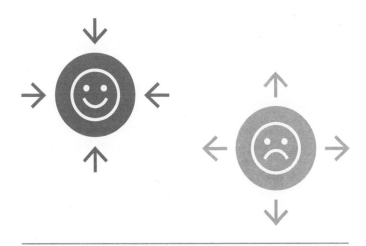

TRUST MATTERS

CLARITY

COMPASSION

CHARACTER

COMPETENCY

COMMITMENT

CONNECTION

CONTRIBUTION

CONSISTENCY

SOLVE WITH TRUST

Three Cheers for Gratitude

One secret and irresistible quality of magnetic people is that they're grateful. Being grateful actually tops the magnetic trait chart above honesty and respectfulness and even being a good listener. *Most of the repelling traits go away automatically for those who have a habit of gratitude.* Grateful people don't tend to be entitled or complainers or poor listeners. You can't be grateful and arrogant at the same time.

You may think expressing thanks is benefitting others—which is true—but research shows it's actually changing *you* for the better! In an article by UCLAHealth.org, we learn that practicing gratitude for fifteen minutes a day "can enhance mental wellness and possibly promote a lasting change in perspective."[72] According to a meta-analysis of seventy different studies done on the association of gratitude and mental health, the University of New England–Australia, concluded with near certainty that the presence of gratitude results in a marked decline in depression and anxiety. "Gratitude can be cultivated and practiced."[73]

Your demeanor makes a big difference in the impact you have on your teams and in your company. Take a moment to read through the following list and reflect on how you may be coming across. Mark an "x" on the continuum between each set of traits for where you are today. It's easy to judge yourself by how you *intend* to be. Visualize your *actual* patterns of words and actions. How would your workplace or family perceive you?

Magnetic Traits	Repelling Traits
Grateful	Thankless
Listener	Talker
Talks about ideas	Talks about others
Optimistic	Pessimistic
Encouraging	Critical
Honest	Exaggerating
Sincere	Fake
Humble	Egotistical
Confident	Arrogant
Respectful	Sarcastic

If you could only choose one trait to practice, which would it be? Once you identify a trait you know needs some attention, consider walking through the Trust Tool #8: How? How? How? to pinpoint an action you can take today to move the needle toward being more magnetic. For example:

How exactly could you become more _____ ?

And then... *how* could you do that? _____

And *how* could you start that? _____

    When exactly? _____

    Where exactly? _____

> *Questions drive conversations.* -DH

Trust Tool #25: CURIOUS QUESTIONS™

A mentor of mine, Patricia Fripp, says, "The key to connection is conversation. The key to conversation is questions." The people asking good questions are some of the smartest ones in the room. Their genuine curiosity makes them interested in connecting and learning from others. Whether at a dinner party or leading an annual review, the power of strategically curious questions will not only lead to clarity, but it will also deepen your relational connections. Thoughtful, intentional conversation can both endear you to the other party AND move your relationship toward depth and solutions.

DISCOVERY?

SOLUTION?

RESULT!

This tool is designed especially for a one-on-one or small group scenario led by a trusted supervisor. Discovery and Solution questions, when sequenced together, carry a coaching conversation from interesting to productive. *The key element throughout the whole flow is a spirit of curiosity.* Your mentee or employee must perceive that you are actively listening and applying what you're hearing in real time.

This takes patience for some of us who often feel we knew the solution before the conversation even started and can't wait to throw it down and walk away. I've certainly done this without meaning to. The beauty of curious conversations is that while you maintain authority as leader, you also maintain integrity and connection with your staff. They have the opportunity to build the solution with you, very often making it better.

Discovery Questions

Discovery questions help uncover everything from hopes and dreams to truth and context. The power of starting with Discovery questions is that it frames your conversation with openness and curiosity. You are gathering information from either the past or present that when pulled to the forefront of your minds will be fodder for the solution. You want the whole experience to be non-threatening. Starting with Discovery questions, while demonstrating you are listening, will give you the best chance of effective engagement.

Discovery Question Examples

- What would a home run look like on this project?

- What is your biggest worry right now?

- What are you loving about this process?

- What is your biggest hope for our new initiative?

The listening is as important as the asking. The key here is to authentically take an interest in others and work to truly hear what they are saying. Ask yourself: "Who is this person?" (as a person, not a boss or coworker) and let your genuine interest lead the conversation.

Solution Questions

As you discover and begin to see the building blocks needed for the solution, there will come a subtle shift to a focus on the future and possible next steps. You've established the facts, so now your Solution questions will take those facts and explore what to do with them. Avoid telling or directing. Intentionally turn thoughts into questions to learn more.

Solution Question Examples

- Who needs to be included on this project to hit a home run?

- What would be the first thing we could do to alleviate that concern?

- How could we leverage this strength to help us reach a solution?

- How can we start getting buy-in for the new initiative?

Practicing this flow from questions about what's working or not to what we can do about it will build trust over time and actually speed up collaborative solutions.

For some who haven't experienced healthy conflict, there can be a tendency to stay in the Discovery questions too long. This can feel safe but is falsely productive and in the end wears everyone out and erodes trust in the process. It can be a delicate navigation, but knowing when it's time to move from the mud to the highway is the leader's job.

> "No one cares
> how much you know
> until they know
> how much you care."
> —President Theodore Roosevelt

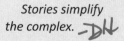
Trust Tool #26: STORYTELLING™

I saw a great saying on the wall as my wife and I entered the International Storytelling Center in Jonesborough, Tennessee. It stated, "Perhaps if we knew everyone's story, there would be no more war."

We could barely hear the tiny old woman who stood on stage all by herself. I had come to Tennessee for the National Storytelling Festival, and I knew this 92-year-old woman must be good based on the reaction of the standing-room-only crowd. Why was everyone so anxious to hear her? The program had given her a prominent space in the schedule, but to me she just looked like an ordinary grandma who might soon need to sit down. As I worried about who would bring her a chair, I began to pick up her words. A genuine Tennessee native, she had lived a real life and was authentic and honest. She saw life through a practical lens, and if you weren't listening carefully, you might miss the dry humor. It was the kind of story you could relate to and the kind that made you love the teller.

I've never lost the lesson I learned that day: *authenticity trumps grandeur.* You can learn how to tell powerful stories, but it's not the timing or the gestures or the outfit that will make them listen as much as the authenticity. If it's *your* story and the *real you* shows through, you will make a solid connection with your audience whether it's your grandchild or your governing board.

If you are leading anything, it's an incredible advantage to be comfortable and competent with the spoken word.

We've all had that spellbound, heart-wrenching experience of listening, reading, or watching a good story. Researchers have found that subjects listening to an engaging story have higher levels of oxytocin, which in turn produces higher levels of empathy.[74] This is why storytelling matters if we want to connect with others.

CEO and Chief Story Facilitator at Leadership Story Lab, Esther Choy, says, "Being a master storyteller is a must-have leadership skill."[75] It's true, I've never met a leader who didn't benefit from communicating well on the platform. It's a skill you can develop and improve!

Storytelling Benefits

Here are five amazing benefits of incorporating good storytelling into your leadership.

1. **Stories simplify the complex.**
   In one short story, I can often shift thinking about trust better than sharing pages of research and data.

2. **Telling stories naturally creates stronger connections.**
   Stories make life and people relatable. Sharing something about yourself is a genuine way to show your human side and foster vulnerability and humility. This does not mean being the hero of the story by sharing your great accomplishments or one-upping what others have shared. Instead, a story of a mistake you made can rapidly build connection.

3. **Stories have power to shape character and culture.**
   For thousands of years, stories have shaped behaviors and cultures. Stories can shape your team. Gritty teams tell stories of how they had to persevere in tough times. Don Soderquist was COO of Walmart in the fast-growing years when they went from $1 billion to $200 billion in revenue.[76] He was known as the "Culture Keeper." It was an honor to stay at his home and be mentored by one of the kindest leaders I have ever met.

When I asked him what drove culture the most, he said, "Storytelling at Saturday morning all-company meetings." As I recall he said, "We told stories of what was going well, shared those stories often, and in turn our people identified with and acted on those stories."

4. **Storytelling fosters a pattern of sharing.**
   Often if someone is willing to start sharing, others will do the same. One of our Trust Edge Certified Coaches always starts meetings by having leaders share a quick story with each other. Even in the toughest, arms-crossed environments, people open up, connect, and start to look forward to the experience.

5. **Stories connect across different cultures.**
   When we share human experience, we connect. If it is something we too have experienced, it instantly draws us together. If the story is different than our experience, we often learn and start to see another perspective. Stories have combatted many "isms" because they help us put our feet in someone else's shoes.

"Perhaps if we knew everyone's story, there would be no more war." —International Storytelling Center

---

If you are leading anything, it's an incredible advantage to be comfortable and competent with the spoken word. Warren Buffet, one of the richest people in the world and the CEO of

Berkshire Hathaway, told Columbia University graduates that public speaking and communication skills are the greatest skills to improve their careers and net worth.[77] Invest in your delivery skills and practice sharing authentic stories. The connection and trust you build will pay off!

Ideas for Improving Storytelling

- Join Toastmasters International, the National Speakers Association, or another speaking-related group.

- Listen to excellent speakers and read good literature.

- Mind map your company values and brainstorm personal stories that relate to each one. You'll be more prepared for an opportune moment. (Visit TrustMattersBook.com/Mindmapping for a video on how to mindmap.)

- Practice! Start incorporating a story at annual meetings or any strategic meeting that needs some life. Use stories to convey the essential points you want them to remember.

- Read *Talk Like TED* by Carmine Gallo.[78] It examines the top-rated TED Talks of all time and shares what they have in common.

- Read *StoryBrand* by my friend, Donald Miller, who gives a road map of the components of all great stories.

- For a real, authentic experience, attend the National Storytelling Festival in Jonesborough, Tennessee, held annually in October.

TRUST MATTERS

CLARITY

COMPASSION

CHARACTER

COMPETENCY

COMMITMENT

*Cut attrition and increase engagement by
answering these two questions* ⎯DK

Trust Tool #27:
ENGAGEMENT STATEMENT™

Help your team members connect and engage specifically with
the significance of their role in the organization. How does
what they do impact the mission or vision? Does their daily
work contribute to the overall outcomes? Of course it needs
to, but have you ever outlined it explicitly? Making that connection is critical. Everyone approaches their work differently
when they see how it matters. Research shows when people
clearly see how they fit the larger purpose and how their
unique contribution fits into that mission, engagement goes up
and people stay longer.[79]

ROLE   MISSION   TASKS

Creating an Engagement Statement

The outcome of this tool is a succinct individual summary distilling job descriptions, mission, and vision into one powerful statement that connects individuals to the big picture.

1. Start with a clear company or group mission statement that relates to everyone.

2. Ask two key questions for each individual:

    *   How does my role/job description help to fulfill our mission?

    *   How do my daily responsibilities contribute to company success?

3. Provide time and examples. This can be harder for some roles than others, so I recommend working individually first and then as a team. Many times, leaders or team members can help others see more clearly how their work affects the whole.

4. Simplicity and brevity are the power of this tool. After doing some wordsmithing, consolidate your answers into the following format:

    I fulfill our mission by _____,

    and I win every day by _____.

5. As a leader, confirm and affirm these statements in a team meeting. It's important to make sure they are accurate AND that your staff hears that you know their work matters. This alignment goes a long way.

6. Encourage people to post their statements on their desks or pin them electronically where they will serve as a daily visual reminder.

It seems incredibly simple, but if your team can answer and understand these two questions, retention will go up and people will more clearly see how they fit into the overall mission of your organization. This in turn drives motivation and engagement. Consider these example Engagement Statements:

Chief of Staff

- *I fulfill the mission by* being the voice of the CEO to the team and taking our strategy from ideas to results.

- *I win every day by* ensuring every team member has clarity on their priorities and accountability on their performance so our missional and financial goals are met and the culture thrives.

Technical Director

- *I fulfill the mission by* solving tech problems so that customers and colleagues can be successful.

- *Every day I win by* pushing tech projects forward and serving our clients and team.

Content Director

- *I fulfill the mission by* aligning all content and publications with the values of our company.

- *I win every day by* producing content that measurably increases our customer base.

When employees operate with this knowledge daily, they frame their work with value and are motivated to engage.

This tool is a part of TELI's One-Voice Framework™. If you'd like more information on organization-wide alignment, visit TrustEdge.com/OneVoice.

Trust Tool #28: THE SOLVING CIRCLE™

Many leaders feel pressure to appear confident and capable of handling any problem. This can lead to a dangerous ignorance trap in which we fail to position ourselves as learners. Once we admit that our own knowledge is limited, we make a way to access what we need.

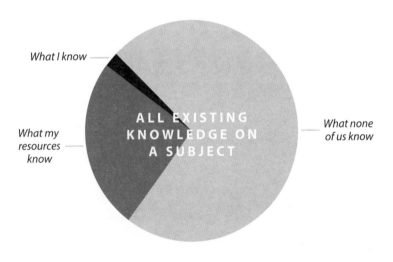

What I know

What my resources know

ALL EXISTING KNOWLEDGE ON A SUBJECT

What none of us know

The goal of the Solving Circle is to help you deal with two problems. First, that your personal knowledge is a small fraction of available knowledge. Second, all of what is unknown is overwhelmingly large but unreachable. Don't be intimidated by either one. *Instead, focus on all the people and resources you can tap into to help you.* That middle piece of the pie is where the answers are found. Leaders who tend to get stuck or fail stay in the "I don't know anything about this" sliver of the circle, or they complain about the biggest part of the pie section: "No one I know can help me with this problem." The key is to jump to the part where you can brainstorm others you could connect with because they might know something about the problem, serve as a resource, or offer another path forward. When we stay in that mindset, we have always found a next step.

Your network knows more than you might think.

Start by writing down the names of five people or resources you could access or connect with around the issue you're facing. Reach out to each one with a set of questions you've prepared ahead of time. Ask questions like:

- Have you ever experienced...?
- What did you do when...?
- How did you solve this problem?
- Do you know anyone I could get advice from?
- Do you know of any resources to help with...?

TRUST MATTERS
CLARITY
COMPASSION
CHARACTER
COMPETENCY
COMMITMENT
CONNECTION
CONTRIBUTION
CONSISTENCY
SOLVE WITH TRUST

At the start of the pandemic in 2020, many individuals were extremely uncertain: "I've never been through this," and "No one knows anything about what to do." However, one leader I know started reaching out to people in their nineties because those seniors had lived through the pandemic of 1918! This leader gained invaluable information that helped form a solution for *that* moment.

Pick up the phone, make a connection, email a connection of a connection, or take some knowledgeable people out for coffee to discuss what's on your mind. Do whatever is possible to learn from others and grow your network *and* your knowledge!

> *Building trust virtually doesn't*
> *have to be so hard.* —DH

Trust Tool #29:
FIVE WAYS TO BUILD VIRTUAL TRUST™

Now that a considerable number of organizations have settled into a hybrid work mode, we need to keep improving how we do this. Connection is even more critical in virtual settings!

TRAINING

REGULARITY

PERSONAL

CLARITY

RESULTS

How do you build trust at a distance? Use these five important components of building trust in a virtual world. See how you are doing with each of them and where you might be able to improve.

Build Virtual Trust

1. **Establish a structure of predictability.**
   Implement systems of check-ins and feedback because things that are communicated casually in person can be frequently missed in a virtual environment. Not knowing what is happening limits trust. One of the biggest frustrations of remote work happens when employees don't know when they will talk to their supervisor next. When remote workers and their managers schedule regular status meetings, both parties can stay on track and aligned while preventing frustration and disengagement from creeping in.

   ❓ *Does everyone have a predictable next meeting with their supervisor?*

2. **Connect personally and professionally.**
   Relating and connecting on personal levels about things happening at home or in other areas in people's lives happens as a matter of course in person, but in virtual environments there is a tendency to get down to business right away. Personal connections are important for establishing trust and for making people feel seen and known as valuable individuals on the team. Connection time can be powerful even while being short. Try this quick five-minute opening: have everyone answer one question, such as what they are most looking forward to in the next few months.

   ❓ *Do you have some time for personal connection of employees every week?*

3. Amplify clarity.

What often seems clear and straightforward to some may not be so to others. The learning and expectations that are transferred informally are never transferred virtually. Goals should be both clear and overcommunicated, otherwise ambiguity sets in, and we lose sight of the target. If a pivot or big initiative needs to be shared, make sure to clearly and consistently communicate the why behind it—especially if you want to keep trust virtually.

❓ *Is everyone crystal clear on what is expected of them in order to be successful?*

4. Emphasize results.

In a remote world, rewarding and compensating on results can take the guesswork and potential skepticism out of the equation. When people are held accountable to clear, previously agreed-upon results, people are happier because they know how to succeed. It is less important if someone clocks in and clocks out after exactly eight hours of work. What is important is that employees meet goals and provide expected results. Trusting people to be responsible for their work—focusing on results—is better for everyone in a hybrid work world.

❓ *Is everyone consistently showing progress on their most critical outcomes?*

TRUST MATTERS

CLARITY

COMPASSION

CHARACTER

COMPETENCY

COMMITMENT

CONNECTION

CONTRIBUTION

CONSISTENCY

SOLVE WITH TRUST

5. Provide hardware, software, and training.

To stay connected, team members need not only the hardware and software to work remotely, but also the knowledge of how to work remotely in an effective way. A responsible work style adapted for the remote environment remains key to establishing trust. A complaint of many hybrid and remote workers is that they are forgotten when it comes to upskilling and development opportunities.

❓ *Does everyone have all they need to perform at their best?*

Connection fosters belonging and fuels personal growth.

Results
matter.

TRUST MATTERS

CLARITY

COMPASSION

CHARACTER

COMPETENCY

COMMITMENT

CONNECTION

CONTRIBUTION

CONSISTENCY

SOLVE WITH TRUST

Pillar 7:
Contribution

People respond to results.

THE CONTRIBUTION PILLAR is about results, outcomes, performance, and impact. Contributing results is the ultimate bottom-line measure of an individual's value to a team or community. This pillar comes near the end of the list because this is where the rubber meets the road.

You can't only be a person of character; you need to actually get things done if you want to be trusted. You may care deeply about your colleagues and be totally competent in your role, but without delivering results, you will lose trust. A pilot might be kind and compassionate, but if he can't fly you from point A to point B safely, you're not getting on the plane. At the end of the day, a teacher needs to actually produce students who have learned something, a dentist has to be able to fill the cavity accurately, a basketball player needs to get the ball in the basket, a law enforcement officer needs to keep the community safe, and a real estate professional needs to get the property sold. You need to achieve the goal, get the result, or provide the outcome if you want to be trusted.

Why Contribution Matters

- *Self-esteem goes up when a person does great work.* When people perform well at work and get excellent outcomes, they trust themselves more.

- *Achieving goals improves job satisfaction.* Being a contributor creates an innate sense of belonging.

- *You can't succeed (or stay) in business without contributing results.* From nonprofits to companies to governments, you are trusted based on your performance.

- *The world's biggest problems cannot be solved without people who work hard and persevere until there is a solution.* Getting results and achieving outcomes signals that you care and are committed.

- *Actions speak louder than words.* People remember what you do far more than they remember what you say. They can tell if someone is all talk.

Changing Expectations

Today's world wants less rhetoric and more results. Don't just promise it; prove it! With increased expectations for performance and accountability, we have a higher demand for data, evidence, and proof of a job well done.

Contribution in the Workplace

When contribution is weak or compromised, you will find disorganization, avoidance of responsibility, or careless follow-through. There may be a lack of focus and often unproductive communication, lack of procedures, too much redundancy, and excessive waste. Deadlines become unreliable, and standards grow shaky. You will likely see a rise of excuses, overwhelmed individuals, more sick days, and poor morale. A 2019 study by BetterUp found that a workplace environment where individuals feel productive and connected can actually decrease employee sick days by 75%![80] One of the best things a leader can do is help employees understand and believe in how important their daily work is within the company's broader mission.

Regardless of your industry, the path to success in your career is heavily dependent on your ability to contribute in tangible ways. You might be able to directly influence the bottom line by cutting costs or generating revenue, or you might make other valuable contributions by improving client relationships, creating a bond within your team, and using your workday efficiently. One of the best things a leader can do is help employees understand and believe in how important their daily work is within the broader company goals and mission.

Value is created through contribution!

TRUST MATTERS

CLARITY

COMPASSION

CHARACTER

COMPETENCY

COMMITMENT

CONNECTION

CONTRIBUTION

CONSISTENCY

SOLVE WITH TRUST

Get the Right Things Done

Many gifted entrepreneurs and visionary leaders have incredible ideas but struggle with how to make their big visions come to life. Two hundred great ideas are worth less than one good idea carried out to completion. According to the Bureau of Labor Statistics, one of every five small businesses fail within their first year and only half survive to five years. They stumble to implement their great ideas.[81]

A person with a strong Contribution Pillar is one who has a bias for action. In both personal and business relationships, there are few things that build trust faster than seeing actual results. Bringing results doesn't only mean getting things done, it means getting the *right* thing done. Action is important, but so is making strategic choices about what to focus on in each stage of implementing the vision. Doing work that matters most is essential for success.

The purest display of trust is
when individuals rely on
each other to do their part.

Collaboration Is a Win-Win

Organizations want results from employees, and employees generally desire to contribute to their organization. Let's face it: winning teams are fun to be on because they *win*! When people see others actively participating and contributing, they are more likely to reciprocate. This mutual exchange fosters a level of collaboration not otherwise possible.

Reward Individual Contributions

When companies value and reward contribution, they retain their top talent. People don't leave jobs because of the paycheck; they leave jobs because they don't feel accomplished or appreciated. Since you tend to get what you reward, reward *results*. In most salaried positions, how and when work gets done doesn't matter as much as the quality and quantity of the output being delivered. Only you know how important this is in your particular industry, but to the extent that you can, reward results over insisting on a certain process or exact timeframe. If it's excellent work, that's what matters!

The Role of the Leader

The role of the leader is to create an environment where people can perform at their best. The leader is the culture keeper and the motivator of desired outcomes. The relationship between contribution and trust is self-reinforcing. It's cyclical. When you contribute and follow through on your responsibilities, it establishes a sense of accountability. When you invite accountability, it pushes you to be better. When you push to be better, others around you will be inspired to do the same. Those on the team who are not consistently contributing at a high level become more noticeable. This is where trusted leaders recognize the need to mentor, communicate, encourage, equip, and teach those who may be struggling to contribute.

> When senior leadership is trusted, employees will offer more ideas and be better team players.

CONTRIBUTION TRUST TOOLS

#30 Difference-Making Actions

#31 Task Bundles

#32 Power Hour

#33 Six Es of Motivation

TRUST MATTERS

CLARITY

COMPASSION

CHARACTER

COMPETENCY

COMMITMENT

CONNECTION

CONTRIBUTION

CONSISTENCY

SOLVE WITH TRUST

> *Get the most important things done every day with DMAs.* —DH

Trust Tool #30:
DIFFERENCE-MAKING ACTIONS™

I once hired a young man right out of college. After three months on the job, he was totally outperforming my expectations. I took one look in his cubicle and discovered the reason. He had around 60 sticky notes, one for each day he'd worked so far, stuck all over the walls. They were the daily Difference-Making Actions he had accomplished each workday. Daily clarity leads to big accomplishments!

Goal: _____

Difference-Making Actions:

1. _____

2. _____

3. _____

4. _____

5. _____

The Difference-Making Actions (DMAs) Trust Tool my young employee was using is the same one many leaders and organizations benefit from today.

Clarity Pillar meets Contribution Pillar on this one. It's the clarity that allows for a narrowing of focus. The inspiration behind DMAs came from Charles Schwab, President of the Bethlehem Steel Company. In the early 1900s, a business consultant named Ivy Lee told Schwab that he could share a strategy with all of Schwab's managers in 15 minutes that would double their productivity. When Schwab inquired about his rates, Lee said, "After using this strategy for six months, you can pay me what you think it's worth." Ivy Lee told Charles Schwab and his managers:

> *What differentiates this from other productivity tools is that David encourages leaders not to attack any other tasks until those five Difference-Making Actions are completed. Brilliant and oh-so-effective!*
> —**Michelle Backes**, Owner of The Savvy U, TELI Senior Consultant

> *Every night, at the end of each day, write down the six most important things that need to get done the next day. Write only six, no more. Prioritize them with number one being the most important. In the morning, start with number one and do only number one until it is completed. Do not go on to number two until number one is completed. When number one is completed go on to number two, then do only number two until it is completed. And so on. If you get done with all of them, you can start a new list.*

After a few months, Lee received a letter and check for $25,000 ($850,000+ in today's money) from the Bethlehem Steel Company! Schwab said in his letter that the 15-minute lesson was the most profitable he had ever learned. Bethlehem Steel went from a struggling little business to a giant in the steel industry.[82]

DMAs is my version of this powerful daily exercise, and many people have said it is their favorite Trust Tool. It can make a palpable difference in your life and work too. I recommend making your DMA list first thing every morning. Our team determines daily DMAs, and individuals briefly share them at our morning stand-up meeting.

List Your DMAs

1. Use a (paper or digital) sticky note.

2. First thing every morning, record your current, most important goal.

3. Write the numbers 1 through 5.

4. Next to the 1, write the single most important action you can take today to achieve that goal, followed by the next most important thing you can do to achieve that goal, and so on.

Many busy leaders have remarked that a deadline of noon keeps them on task. After lunch, they can respond to whatever else comes up without interfering with their most crucial progress.

Guidelines

Follow these guidelines to bring clarity to the day's TOP priority and the very specific steps you can take to work on or complete that priority:

☐ ***Focused.*** This is not a to-do list with all your tasks for the week. There should be no more than five tasks, and they all should directly relate to the top goal. If you can't distill down your current, most important goal to a few simple tasks, you probably need to go back and refocus the goal. Once you have a list of your most critical actions, build your day around them. Prioritize them over meetings, communications, and other tasks.

☐ ***Clear and Measurable.*** You can't always control the outcomes, but you can control what you are going to do. *Always* attach a number to your DMA so it is measurable. For example, "Spend two hours on the proposal" is much clearer than "Work on the proposal." These are DMAs because they have a number: "Review four contracts" or "Write three thank-you notes." The number allows you to know when it's complete. Without a number attached, it is not a DMA.

☐ ***Realistic.*** Your DMAs won't make any difference if you can't actually complete them. DMAs should only consist of tasks you can accomplish without being reliant on someone else. For example, a DMA could be to "Make five calls" but shouldn't be to "Talk to five people." You can make the calls but can't guarantee someone will pick up the phone. Be certain each task is *achievable* that same day. Practicing DMAs regularly will teach you what is realistic; it may also reveal some time usage patterns that are inhibiting your contributions. Make your task list realistic and make it a habit to get them done. Solid contribution is the best feeling!

> *Bundle your tasks to*
> *get more done!* —DH

Trust Tool #31: TASK BUNDLES™

Imagine you had to bake three dozen cookies. Would you
bake them one at a time? Of course not! But that's exactly
how some people approach their work. They make a phone
call, write an email, then switch back to the phone, work on a
proposal, and so on. We've all succumbed to this counterpro-
ductive method. It forces your mind to switch gears more often
than necessary and wastes time with each shift.

Steps to Bundle Tasks

Allowing yourself to be sporadic is a tendency that can be overcome. To start, examine your daily workload and decide what tasks would be most efficiently accomplished together.

1. **Start with the obvious.**

   Phone calls, emails, and paperwork are prime candidates to be grouped together. In most cases, they can be done more quickly and efficiently in a batch rather than one at a time.

   For changes specific to your work life, look through your calendar for other tasks that make sense to group together. Keep an eye toward saving time, and you're bound to find at least a few options.

2. **Set a time limit.**

   Give yourself a deadline—30 minutes for example—to finish the batch of jobs. This will keep you focused on getting through them without stalling or procrastinating.

   Consider designating a time period each day when you ask your team or manager for no interruptions. Your colleagues can help protect your time while you accomplish your tasks. Be sure to reciprocate for them as well. (See the next tool for a concrete plan you could try!)

3. **Stay in your seat.**

   When you start working on a group of tasks, decide that you will finish them before you get up to do anything else. It will help you concentrate and finish faster. Resist the urge to distract yourself by stepping away from the tasks at hand.

4. Reflect and revise.

Ask yourself:

- Did that feel good?

- Did I give enough time to it?

- Did my bundle of tasks make sense?

- Will I eventually become more efficient if I keep trying this method?

- Is there another bundle I should try?

Meeting Day

If possible, a great way to get through your meetings is to bundle them by category. Having them back-to-back means it's easier to stay in the right mindset. Additionally, you will have a good reason to keep each one to the point. Alternatively, you could have a meeting-*free* day. Set aside one day a week in which you do not schedule or accept any meetings, so you can complete your tasks. I really like to set aside longer uninterrupted periods of time when I need to focus on big projects.

> *Uninterrupted focused time*
> *multiplies output.* -DN

Trust Tool #32: POWER HOUR™

Writing down your Difference-Making Actions is one thing but getting them done is another. Despite our best intentions, we all know how quickly those priorities can be pushed aside to deal with urgent tasks and interruptions.

In my office and in many others, having a Power Hour has been a great way to accomplish what is most important. It's so simple; you might be surprised at how well it works. For a predetermined, 60-minute block of time each morning, our office doesn't take any interruptions at all. No meetings, no conversations, no phone calls, and no emails, everyone, all at the same time. Emails go to the inbox, and phone calls go to voicemail or to someone designated to have their Power Hour at another time. For that one hour, focus on the activities you have identified as top priorities for your role.

How to Make a Power Hour Work

1. Go public.

Let everyone you work with know you are setting aside an hour a day at a certain time. Informing assistants, customers, and colleagues of your plans will make them less likely to disturb you.

2. Share the idea.

In my office, *everyone* gets a Power Hour at the same time. That way, we don't interrupt each other, and we all get more done.

3. Be consistent.

Use the same time every day if you can. It will allow people who work with you to get used to your routine and help reinforce the habit in your mind. It can be hard to protect the Power Hour when you or others are traveling but do your best within the constraints of your positions to be as consistent as you can.

If one hour is good, is two better? Maybe for you. In our experience, 60 minutes is long enough to get something significant done but short enough to keep your sense of urgency. If anything, perhaps designate a second Power Hour later in the afternoon.

Still skeptical? Try it at home on the weekends first. You will find that your most dreaded tasks, the ones that taint your entire weekend because you don't want to do them, don't actually take all that long. Whether at home or at work, I guarantee you will be surprised at how much you can accomplish in just 60 minutes. Not only will you make headway on your biggest projects, but you will also find that by getting the day off to a strong start, you will often feel energized to accomplish more in your remaining time.

Results speak louder than words or actions.

TRUST MATTERS

CLARITY

COMPASSION

CHARACTER

COMPETENCY

COMMITMENT

CONNECTION

CONTRIBUTION

CONSISTENCY

> *Keep your people motivated toward*
> *the right results.* ⎼DH

Trust Tool #33: SIX Es OF MOTIVATION™

People are motivated in two main ways: *toward* or *away from*. Motivation toward a goal is generally best, but how do you motivate a team when some want challenging work, some want bonuses, and some want more time off? There are leaders who resort to negative motivators like embarrassment, withdrawal, or demotion, but effective leaders find creative and positive ways to motivate their team through a multi-faceted approach.

EXAMPLE

EXPECTATION

EDUCATION

ENCOURAGE

EMPOWER

EXTEND TRUST

Effective Motivation

Utilize these six core fundamentals of motivation to encourage individuals on your team to make big contributions.

E1 – Example

People mimic the behavior they see. Actions speak louder than words. Model the level of contribution you are expecting from others. Avoid coming across as a superstar which can backfire. Let your people hear you process what motivates you and see you jump in to contribute.

E2 – Expectation

How can your team contribute consistently if the expectations are unclear or intermittent? People tend to step up to what is expected of them. Make your expectations clear and deliver them with an explanation of why it matters to the team goals. I had two very different coaches growing up. One expected greatness; the players gave him greatness. The other expected us to lose; that's what we did. Expect the best, and you just might get it!

E3 – Education

Do your employees know the most efficient and effective methods to do their job well? It can be really motivating to be well trained. An employee who knows they are equipped with the latest and best is excited to contribute. Be thorough at onboarding and periodically review your education opportunities to keep motivation high. People are motivated to change behavior when they are educated on a topic. When I learned the impact of certain foods on my body, I stopped eating them.

E4 – Encourage

Encouragement is golden, and no one gets enough of it. There's nothing like a sincere and well-timed compliment. It takes awareness but hardly any time at all. The interesting thing about encouragement is that giving it often works almost as well as getting it. Encouragement goes a long way.

I will never forget a big day of bailing hay on the farm when I was 14 years old. It was hard work throwing 50-pound bales of hay onto the wagons. Sunup to sundown we didn't stop because rain was in the forecast. We got back home late that night with over 1,000 bales safe in the barn just as the rain started to fall. My mom came running out to tell us there was hot food ready to eat. My dad shut off the tractor and shouted across the yard and through the rain, "Look what your son did today." What an incredible feeling. I immediately felt like Superman! My father's way of encouraging a job well done is part of the reason many people loved working for him.

E5 – Empower

When you empower others, it leads to an overall multiplier of contribution. If you are the top leader, make it a practice to empower your leaders publicly, so that the entire team expects and yields to their developing leadership.

There are two types of empowerment:

- providing the resources needed to do the job effectively, and

- publicly affirming the leaders who are appointed.

E6 – Extending Trust

There is an inherent risk associated with extending trust. This should be done with discernment, and it can take time to build, but it's critical to team success. Extending trust to others can be a great motivator for innovation and productivity. Often people will step up to the task when they are trusted with something important. Those who never take the risk are never rewarded.

Trusted people achieve results.

Predictability matters.

Pillar 8: Consistency

People are wired to identify patterns and predict behaviors.

IMAGINE A MAN with huge muscles and no fat, and you will get a picture of my bodybuilding friend, Kevin! He was preparing for a physique competition and sticking to his rigorous nutrition and workout regimen when everything changed. On January 12, 2017, Kevin's vehicle was hit by a Range Rover that blew through a stop light at 50 miles per hour. The surgeons said he would have died immediately, but the muscle mass on his chest saved him! Kevin went into a coma, had five hip fractures, eight broken ribs, a deflated lung, and a broken scapula, among other injuries. After 42 days, Kevin miraculously woke up without any brain damage, but he was 66 pounds lighter!

Sometimes, when I share this story at events, I show the before and after picture of Kevin because it is a stunning visual of the power of atrophy. Through no fault of his own, Kevin's well-developed muscles atrophied because he was unable to eat, move, exercise, or lift weights. It is THE SAME with trust. *Unless you are actively building trust every day, atrophy will set in.* Consistency is what builds the muscle, the habit, the marriage, the reputation, the brand, and even the health and vibrancy of a workplace!

In a world where change is constant and options are endless, consistency helps individuals and brands stand out, build trust, and maintain relevance.

Why Consistency Matters

- *Good ideas and great intentions become irrelevant without consistency.* Basically, no word, action, or behavior is impressive if it's every once in a while.

- *Repetitive patterns become the preferred pathways.* Whether neurons in the brain or waterways in the Grand Canyon, the power of repetition is irrefutable.

- *Inconsistency can undermine all other good work.* Brands and reputations are only as strong as the consistency of the experience.

- *You increase or decrease trust through every single interaction.* Trust is never static. Every transaction, every conversation, every encounter either builds it or weakens it.

- *Predictability lowers stress and provides emotional security.* Think of the most reliable person you know. It's not stressful to be around them, right? That is because predictability naturally lowers stress!

Consistency Is the Glue

Consistency multiplies the strength of every other pillar. It's like the chemical reaction of epoxy glue that requires two parts to be combined to be effective. By themselves, the pillars are each strong and have their unique place, but activating them with consistency multiplies the impact.

Pillar 1: **Clarity**
Pillar 2: **Compassion**
Pillar 3: **Character**
Pillar 4: **Competency**
Pillar 5: **Commitment**
Pillar 6: **Connection**
Pillar 7: **Contribution**

X Pillar 8: **Consistency** **=** **LASTING TRUST**

For example:

- *Clarity + Consistency:* A clear mission statement still fails if not communicated consistently.

- *Competency, Compassion, or Character + Consistency:* Being competent, compassionate, or displaying great character in a moment is noticed but not fully trusted until it's consistent.

- *Commitment + Consistency:* Commitment without consistency is not commitment.

- *Connection + Consistency:* An inconsistent value of connecting is like bad cell phone reception—unreliable!

- *Contribution + Consistency:* If you deliver results sometimes but not consistently, it will erode trust.

Three Types of Consistency

1. Personal Consistency

This is your reputation. People want to know you are going to show up the same way every time. When a person is strong in the Consistency Pillar, they are reliable and have a certain amount of discipline. They benefit from the sense of security and confidence their colleagues and family members have come to lean on.

When your actions and words align *occasionally*, you are viewed as inauthentic and untruthful. When your actions and words align *consistently*, you are seen as credible and trustworthy.

Am I perceived as being personally consistent?

2. Culture Consistency

Strong cultures make decisions by values that are defined across the organization. Your culture is only as strong as how consistently your purpose and values are displayed.

Researchers at Gallup remind us that culture has impact when "it aligns with your company's values, provides a consistent employee experience, brings the mission and purpose of your organization to life, and delivers on the promises you make to your customers."[83]

Is our culture perceived as consistent?

3. Brand or Product Consistency

Brands are only as strong as the predictability they create. People long for the same experience and quality every time. You can even trust a company you don't like if they give you the same outcome every time.

Anyone who owns a business knows how important it is to create consistency in their branding. How many hundreds of different ways has Target used their red and white symbol? Dogs, dresses, furniture, repeating designs, but all reinforcing the same red and white logo!

When my favorite, long-time NBC sports announcer, Bob Costas, retired, I struggled to love the Olympic coverage quite as much since his voice had become synonymous with the Olympics. For many, his almost 30 years of prime-time coverage was part of the experience. It's not just the visuals and sounds that communicate consistency, the products themselves must provide a consistent experience too.

> *Is our brand perceived as consistent? Is our product perceived as consistent?*

None of your efforts will move the needle on trust if you do not do them consistently.

Focus on Repeaters

I like to describe the magic of the Consistency Pillar by describing the effects of *repeaters*. In a computer network, repeaters are devices that amplify or regenerate an incoming signal before retransmitting it. They are also known as signal boosters.[84] When we are working toward a goal, we can boost our likelihood of accomplishing it by focusing on the repetitive actions that will get us there. It's the little things done consistently that make the big difference.

TRUST MATTERS

CLARITY

COMPASSION

CHARACTER

COMPETENCY

COMMITMENT

CONNECTION

CONTRIBUTION

CONSISTENCY

SOLVE WITH TRUST

Consistent kindness makes a thoughtful person; consistent sales activities make a great salesperson; consistent client experiences make a strong brand. Consistent workouts and nutritious eating make a healthy body. Consistent character, even when no one is watching, makes a leader of integrity.

Consistency multiplies impact.

CONSISTENCY TRUST TOOLS

#34 SEEDS

#35 Habit Change

#36 Brand Review

#37 Brand Balance

TRUST MATTERS

CLARITY

COMPASSION

CHARACTER

COMPETENCY

COMMITMENT

CONNECTION

CONTRIBUTION

CONSISTENCY

SOLVE WITH TRUST

> *To accomplish BIG things, start with these small things.* —DH

Trust Tool #34: SEEDS™

Healthy people tend to make healthy leaders. The state of your mind, body, and relationships influences your abilities. I have often watched people get excited and motivated to do something great, yet they fail because they have not first planted and cultivated their SEEDS. Even though you have heard these principles before, it's the memorable and actionable nature of this tool that makes it so powerful.

SLEEP

EXERCISE

EAT RIGHT

DRINK WATER

SOURCE OF STRENGTH

Nurture Your SEEDS

Just as planted seeds grow best when the soil is cultivated, watered, and fertilized, the following human SEEDS also need daily attention. It's the repetition of these core needs that builds the strong foundation you can leap from to accomplish amazing things. Without addressing them daily, I have found it very difficult to attempt a big change or challenge.

S – Sleep

Have you heard people brag about how little sleep they need? When did good sleep become a measure of how much you're *not* getting done? We might need varying amounts of sleep, but all humans need regular sleep. Figure out how much your body needs and take steps to regulate this aspect of your life. Sleep affects everything from motivation and waistlines to anger levels and productivity.

E – Exercise

Our bodies and minds were designed to work together. Movement activates body systems that do so many good things for your whole being. Inactivity leads to poor health, lack of focus, and lethargy. I have learned when I move a little more, it makes a huge difference!

Think of what YOU are willing to do. I was not going to start running marathons like my wife has, but when I learned I could walk more, it changed my life. Walking led to easy exercises with a few small weights, which led to a pull-up bar on the back door of our home. Sometimes it is as simple as getting a stand-up desk, walking during lunch, taking the stairs, stopping at the gym a couple times a week, or parking at the back of the lot.

E – Eat right

My doctor said to me, "You have to decide if you want to drive a Ferrari or a junker. You put different fuel in a Ferrari. What kind of fuel are you putting into your human machine?" I learned if I fuel my body with green vegetables and some lean protein every day, my body runs much better. I now have a bag of celery in my briefcase while I travel, so I don't eat as many other snacks. Not sure where to start? Try cutting back on your sugar and processed foods.

D – Drink water

Your body is mostly made of water, yet most of us struggle to get enough. It's estimated that 75% of Americans are chronically dehydrated, so clearly, many of us struggle with this.[85] Your body needs enough water to be alert and healthy. Here's one idea that worked for me: first thing after I wake up in the morning, I drink two big glasses of water. In my office, I have a large, favorite glass that I fill up upon arrival. Sometimes, a new reusable water bottle can help motivate the new habit.

S – Source of strength

I have found that employees are better at work when they have a source of strength beyond their work. It could be found in faith, family, or friendships. If you are only getting life from your work, that is not a renewable energy!

Coach Tom Landry, the legendary coach of the Dallas Cowboys, was someone I looked up to when I was growing up. He was strong but kind and was known for having the respect and love of those close to him even during the losing seasons.

(Hint: if you want to know the character of a leader, ask those closest to them, not the far-removed fans.) Landry's calmness in conflict stood out in the high-pressure, public life of an NFL coach. How did he stay so steady when other coaches lost everything from their temper to their families? One reason might have been that he lived by a set of priorities; they were his source of strength. At the beginning of every season, Landry reminded himself of his priorities: God, family, then football, and in that order. When he lost a game, he had a lot left over!

Do you have priorities beyond work? Do you have community outside of work? Humans are made for community, and studies show that having close friends and community helps people live happier, more fulfilled, and longer lives. Bad habits are often formed in isolation. With a friend, we might eat a bowl of ice cream. Alone, we might eat the whole pint. If you want to be better at work, make sure you have a source of strength beyond your work!

> " SEEDS is simple but so powerful. After hearing David walk through it at our recent conference, I immediately went to my clients, coach mentees, even my nieces, to discuss the application of this Trust Tool. It's a reminder that taking care of ourselves is critical to success.
>
> —**Margaret Maclay,** Business Leadership Coach, Global Coach Success Director and Coach Mentor, FocalPoint "

The beauty of this tool is its simplicity. Memorize the acronym and when you find yourself not doing well, check your SEEDS first. If you really want to change one in particular, the next Trust Tool can help.

> *Almost no one ever changes a difficult habit. Here's how.* —DH

Trust Tool #35: HABIT CHANGE™

Consistent behavior allows those around you to predict how you will act in various situations. If positive behaviors are repeated, they will become ingrained in your character. If negative behaviors are repeated, they will become your character. Behaviors, good or bad, quickly become habits!

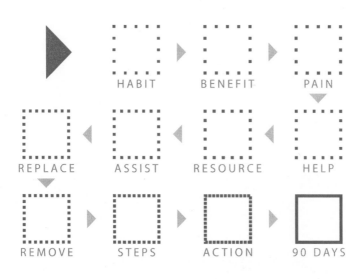

HABIT → BENEFIT → PAIN

REPLACE ← ASSIST ← RESOURCE ← HELP

REMOVE → STEPS → ACTION → 90 DAYS

Steps to Change a Habit

Answer every question in order to increase your chance of changing an old habit for the better:

1. What habit do I want to change?

2. How will I benefit from changing?

3. What pain will I face from not changing?

4. What am I replacing this habit with?

5. What resources or assistance do I need?

6. Who could help me with this habit?

7. What distractions do I need to remove?

8. What specific steps will I take?

9. What will trigger me to take action that I am not currently taking?

10. How can I reward target behavior?

11. How can I keep it top of mind?

12. In 90 days, what will my new habit be?

My friend wanted to write a little bit every day. He bought a printed calendar so he could mark off the days he made time to write, even if just a little bit. Each day, he put a big "x" on the day when he was done writing. He said, "Writer's block is not an excuse for a writer. Writers write, and that's what I will do." My friend loved seeing the visual reminder of his accomplishment on his refrigerator so much that he never wanted to have an empty space on his calendar again. It motivated him to start a streak. Last I checked with him, it had yet to be broken, and his passion for writing has only gotten stronger.

Another example of rewarding or motivating target behavior is to use certain apps like WinStreak. I'm using Duolingo right now and, like most apps, it measures and rewards daily progress and reminds you regularly how long of a streak you have going. Likewise, it uses gentle reinforcement tactics if you miss a day: "Don't lose your streak!" Gamification can reward and encourage consistency and habit change as long as getting on your phone doesn't distract you from your ultimate goal.

Every streak starts with Day 1!

TRUST MATTERS

CLARITY

COMPASSION

CHARACTER

COMPETENCY

COMMITMENT

CONNECTION

CONTRIBUTION

CONSISTENCY

SOLVE WITH TRUST

Trust Tool #36: BRAND REVIEW™

Consistency is what creates an individual's reputation and a company's brand awareness. Ultimately your brand is determined not by slogans or marketing campaigns but by *what you deliver day in and day out.* One way to determine if your brand or reputation is staying aligned with your mission or values is to conduct a Brand Review (individual or corporate) every 90 days.

REPEAT	FEEDBACK	ESSENCE
STRENGTH	MISALIGNED	ACTION

Block some time every 90 days for this quick reflection. If doing a team or corporate Brand Review, you may want to put the questions into a digital form that everyone on your team can submit anonymously. Remember, never do this without sharing the results with the team. There's no sense in gathering information if you aren't going to make good use of it! If doing a personal Brand Review, perhaps you keep a journal (digital or paper) where you answer these basic questions every three months. This simple process can ensure that you never stray too far from the self-aware state you need to succeed.

Reputation Reflection

For Individuals: *Complete on your own.*

1. What traits do I consistently portray?

2. Have I received compliments or complaints about how I do things?

3. What would others say I am all about?

4. What positive reputation do I have?

5. Where am I (either in reality or in perception) misaligned with my Personal Mission Statement or Decision-Making Values?

6. What one consistent action can I focus on in the next 90 days to improve my reputation?

Brand Alignment Review

Corporate: *Complete as a team.*

1. How did we consistently come across to those we served?

2. What feedback have we received that is either positive or negative?

3. What would our customers, clients, patients, students, or stakeholders say we are all about?

_____

_____

4. Where is our brand consistently strong?

_____

_____

5. Where are we (either in reality or in perception) misaligned with our Mission or Values?

_____

_____

6. What one consistent action can we take in the next 90 days to strengthen our brand alignment?

_____

_____

Trust Tool #37: BRAND BALANCE™

Brand expression is an excellent place for consistency. A brand
is more than a name; it's an organizational identity. It's a way of
operating that your clients or customer base come to know and
depend on. The more clearly you can define your brand, the more
consistency will be possible. Get clarity by recognizing that there is a
spectrum your brand falls within.

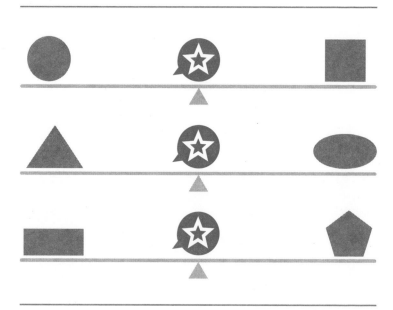

Many marketing experts push people to create their brand by simply coming up with five words that describe their entity. Start there, but then go deeper with this teeter-totter balancing approach. I have found strong brands are more clearly defined when there is a tension between two seemingly opposing concepts. Think of what you want to be known for, then think of how that attribute should be balanced out by another word on the other side of the continuum.

Use Tension to Define Your Brand

Here are some examples of Brand Balance:

Research-Based	*yet*	Actionable
	▲	
Reliable	*yet*	Fun
	▲	
Timeless	*yet*	Modern
	▲	
Thorough	*yet*	Succinct
	▲	
Planned	*yet*	Flexible
	▲	

Have fun coming up with examples. This exercise can help define a company-wide brand, but it can also be used in a small department or team to help differentiate your identity in the workplace.

We make decisions by our Brand Balance almost every day. Take the book that you are holding. It is hard cover and beautifully designed with color. These features are uncommon

TRUST MATTERS

CLARITY

COMPASSION

CHARACTER

COMPETENCY

COMMITMENT

CONNECTION

CONTRIBUTION

CONSISTENCY

SOLVE WITH TRUST

for business books, but that is because we are balancing our brand values: "Research-Based" and "Excellent Quality" with "Fun" and "Actionable." We want this book to feel trusted and, in this attention-span-deprived culture, we also want it to be engaging on every page. This book is a reflection of our brand balance and similar to the other TELI products. It is not right or wrong; it is who *we* are!

Brand alignment is critical for any group that wants to create common experiences and make consistent decisions. The more definitive you can be, the easier it will be for your people to buy in and represent the brand.

You are the sum of the *actions* you take and the *decisions* you make.

Trust is always at the root.

TRUST MATTERS

CLARITY

COMPASSION

CHARACTER

COMPETENCY

COMMITMENT

CONNECTION

CONTRIBUTION

CONSISTENCY

Solve with Trust

How to solve a trust issue in yourself,
in your organization, and during change.

GROWING UP ON A FARM, I saw healthy things grow and sick things die. It's a simple law of nature that cannot be ignored. Plants that don't get enough water will not grow. Weak animals get sick easily. Strong marriages thrive and wounded ones can end in divorce.

Flourishing, trusted cultures don't just happen accidentally. They must be cared for, rooted in the right things, receive proper investment, and be maintained to prevent trust gaps. At TELI, we have seen the effectiveness of the 8-Pillar Framework and these Trust Tools over decades of work. My hope is that you can use this book as a resource to reference again and again. Use it to maintain the health of your own trustworthy leadership and the ongoing vitality of your organization.

Trust Yourself

The globally recognized Golden Rule or ethics of reciprocity can be stated as "Love your neighbor as yourself."[86] If you can't love yourself, you will have a hard time loving others. *It is the same with trust.* If you can't trust yourself, you will have a hard time building trust with others.

I've had the opportunity over the years to interview many leaders who have used our material and Trust Tools with great success. They all say that the work had to start with themselves. Building trust with yourself requires honesty, humility, and work, but it's the essential foundation for any other trusted relationship.

Of course, the last thing I would want to promote is the idea that you should *act* trustworthy in order to receive the benefits of being trusted without actually *being* trustworthy. Does it happen? It happens all the time. Does it end well? Never. You don't have to be perfect, but if you don't (or can't) trust yourself in a healthy way, others won't be able to trust you either. Start with building trust in yourself. (Visit MeasureMyTrust.com for info on how to do a brief trust audit on yourself.)

Solve with Trust

Before you launch into applying this trust work, I have three final points with corresponding tools that apply to everyone. These three tools help bring this trust work together. First, we have to be able to trust ourselves, otherwise how can we expect others to trust us? Second, the process for identifying the counterforces of trust has been invaluable for solving with trust in organizations. Finally, change is hard, yet now is *the* time you can build trust the fastest. Don't overlook how to build trust in crisis.

FINAL TRUST TOOLS

TRUST MATTERS

CLARITY

COMPASSION

CHARACTER

COMPETENCY

COMMITMENT

CONNECTION

CONTRIBUTION

CONSISTENCY

SOLVE WITH TRUST

> *If you can't trust yourself, you can't build it with others.* –DH

Trust Tool #38:
THE GREAT EIGHT FOR SELF-TRUST™

There is no quick fix for becoming trustworthy. There's also no short-cut to a culture of trust without the individuals themselves becoming *worthy* of trust. It takes work, but it's work that is worth it!

HABITS　　　INPUTS　　　CONSISTENCY

PROMISES　　　ENCOURAGERS

PRINCIPLES　　　GENEROUS　　　WORK

The Great Eight

1. Build good habits.

Good habits have countless benefits, but one of them is self-trust. When individuals make good choices, self-trust goes up; when they make bad choices, it goes down. Good habits are a series of good choices, multiplying trust in self.

Start small and progress to challenges that take more discipline and work. As you accomplish more, your trust in your abilities will grow. People who are willing and disciplined trust themselves more. Revisit Trust Tool #35: Habit Change in the Consistency Pillar.

2. Choose good inputs.

If you intentionally keep your mind and heart full of material that encourages and inspires you to be trustworthy, you will more likely see it come to fruition. What we focus on influences our desires which motivates our actions. When we put good things into our mind and body, we believe in ourselves more. Read good books. Listen to good podcasts. Eat good food. Be around good conversation. Watch movies that inspire. Take a deeper dive with Trust Tool #16: Input = Output in the Competency Pillar.

3. Be consistent.

Is there an area where being inconsistent is weighing on you? First dig into the root cause and remove any potential barriers. Then commit to a new plan that will enable you to win. Inserting consistency into any good thing will build trust in yourself. People who are haphazard and make decisions on a whim are less trusted by themselves and others. Take a deeper dive with Trust Tool #34: SEEDS in the Consistency Pillar.

4. **Make and keep promises.**

If you don't keep promises with yourself, you are eroding trust in your own mind. If this becomes a habit, over time, you will lose your perspective of commitments entirely. First, stop overcommitting. Once you've made a realistic commitment, keep it, then celebrate the win. Do it again and again to build your capacity and demonstrate to yourself that you are a promise keeper.

5. **Be around people who believe in you.**

Growing up, I had a coach who believed in me. I stepped up and became so much more because of his influence. If you intentionally spend time with people who encourage you to be your best, you increase your chances of exactly that. Find a few friends who spur you on toward good rather than drag you down. Be intentional about keeping company with others who value trust and who value you.

6. **Be principled.**

Making decisions according to a framework rather than a whim leads to building deeper trust in yourself. People who pre-decide how they will respond before the next crisis hits, before peer pressure mounts, or before fatigue sets in, make it easier for themselves to handle those tough circumstances. Take a deeper dive with Trust Tool #13: Decision-Making Values in the Character Pillar.

7. Serve with generosity.

People who sacrifice for the good of all feel better about themselves. Volunteer, serve, and contribute for your own good, and you will increase trust in yourself. Philanthropic causes always need help so make time to contribute to one that's meaningful to you.

8. Do the work.

Even though you may not feel like doing the work, few things bring greater satisfaction than effort and completion. Building trust takes time and energy but is worth it. People who have a habit of embracing difficult work tend to trust themselves more. You never know how much you're capable of until you have to do something extremely difficult—and you survive. Do hard things and you will grow your capacity to trust yourself.

How to Start

- *Choose one area at a time.* A key to building trust in yourself is to work progressively and set yourself up for wins.

- *Don't be too hard on yourself.* Self-condemnation is only going to stifle your growth and limit your reach.

> From personal relationships to
> financial institutions, everything
> of value is built on trust.

TRUST MATTERS

CLARITY

COMPASSION

CHARACTER

COMPETENCY

COMMITMENT

CONNECTION

CONTRIBUTION

CONSISTENCY

SOLVE WITH TRUST

Trust in Your Organization

Building trust in yourself builds the capacity for you to lead with trust in your team or organization. TELI's ongoing research shows that *every* issue, whether major or minor, falls under one or more of the 8 Pillars of Trust. Avoid a temporary fix or the appearance of a solution by digging down to the root pillar.

What Is a Lack of Trust Costing You?

There is a million-dollar question that can get to truth and launch any team into solving with trust. When team members focus on this question with openness and grit, they are set up to tackle the most important issues that affect impact, success, and even the bottom line.

I ask a question every time I guide a team through strategic planning because it leads to solving the most important issues. That question is: *What is a lack of trust costing our team right now?* If your big problem is attrition, focus on that. If it is sales, focus on that. If it is disengagement, focus on the Pillars of Trust that will solve for that. If we can't be honest about the issue, it's impossible to solve it. Use Trust Tool #8: How? How? How? in the Clarity Pillar to define the most direct pathway to a solution.

Contextualize the Pillars

Whether in another hemisphere or just across town, every group or organization has its own culture or set of norms and expectations. The pillar concepts are universally applicable, but the order you address them in or the way you communicate them might need adjustment based on culture and context.

The most trusted way to show you are listening to someone in North American culture is generally to look the person in the eye. In other parts of the world, listening might be most respectful while avoiding eye contact. So, while listening builds compassion, which builds trust, *how* we listen might change based on context.

In Scandinavian cultures, the Contribution Pillar often trumps the Connection Pillar to start. Getting a result or being productive is more valued than having a face-to-face personal conversation in certain work environments. In South American cultures however, it would often be rude to move straight to a task before establishing a human connection with conversation. This doesn't mean Scandinavians don't want to connect or that South Americans don't want results. It means *how* we build trust and reach goals may take contextualizing the Pillars of Trust appropriately. Dr. Stephan Ruppert explains, "Task-oriented cultures typically build trust at work via competency, facts, and figures as well as objective presentations, while in relationship-oriented cultures trust is established via personal relationships."[87]

Here are some prompts for examining how to best build trust in your organization's culture and in today's globally diverse society:

- Consider who will be most impacted by your efforts to build trust.

- Detail the cultures (and subcultures) present and active.

- Is trust built primarily with tasks or relationships in that culture?

TRUST MATTERS

CLARITY

COMPASSION

CHARACTER

COMPETENCY

COMMITMENT

CONNECTION

CONTRIBUTION

CONSISTENCY

SOLVE WITH TRUST

- How will the accepted cultural communication patterns affect your efforts to build trust?

- View each pillar through a cultural grid.

- What needs adjustment to get the right message across?

- What is the accepted pathway for showing compassion?

- How would this culture define high character?

- How is accountability received in this culture?

- How should feedback be offered or received in this culture?

- What does a guarantee of commitment look like in this culture?

After working across six continents, I have found that no matter the cultural context, *the 8 Pillars of Trust remain the universal traits of trusted people and organizations* around the world. Core issues always fall under clarity, compassion, character, competency, commitment, connection, contribution, or consistency.

TRUST MATTERS

CLARITY

COMPASSION

CHARACTER

COMPETENCY

COMMITMENT

CONNECTION

CONTRIBUTION

CONSISTENCY

> *Identify the gap to pick
> the right pillar.* -DH

Trust Tool #39:
COUNTERFORCE WHEEL

There are many counterforces that compete or fight with the
pillars of trust. The counterforces answer the question: *What
works against this pillar?* Wherever you find these counterforces, you know you must work to limit the erosion of
that pillar.

It's critical to recognize the counterforces that frequently
work against the 8 Pillars of Trust. When you understand and
recognize what you are up against, you can identify the corresponding pillar and focus on making it stronger. For example,
understanding that complexity pushes against clarity, fear dis-
ables commitment, and low expectations tarnish contribution
will help prioritize and solve the real issue faster.

The presence of counterforces isn't necessarily a reflection of poor leadership. The real test comes in how you handle
these negative forces. Use a targeted approach to build up the
pillar that is suffering the most.

COUNTERFORCE WHEEL™

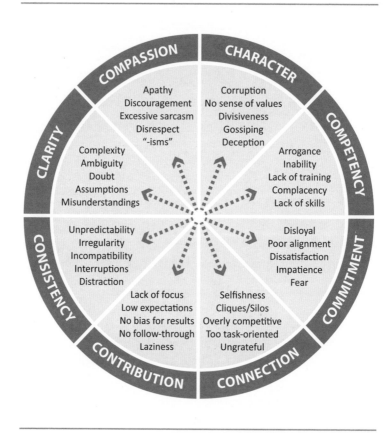

Using the Counterforces Wheel

1. Read through the counterforces for each pillar represented in the graphic.

2. Circle the top three counterforces that you see present in your work or with your team.

3. Identify which pillar you most need to strengthen.

4. Reference that pillar chapter and the Trust Tool Index in the back of the book for solutions.

5. Discuss with your team the best pathway to eliminate or minimize these counterforces and strengthen the pillar.

6. Ask How? How? How? until someone will take a specific action today or tomorrow.

Don't let counterforces derail your success.

How we respond to counterforces or any type of adversity can build or destroy trust faster than any other time. When was George W. Bush the most trusted as President of the United States? His ratings were the highest (90%) the week after 9/11.[88] Times of crisis present your greatest opportunity to build trust.

Trust in Change

A culture of trust not only prepares you on a personal level for change, but it also increases your organization's ability to weather significant change. Humans are built with the capacity for change even though they often fear it. All the pillars work together to build trust, but three rise to the top during times of change: Clarity, Consistency, and Connection.

Clarity in Times of Change

The more uncertain the situation, the more important clarity becomes. When I asked a friend who had served in the military how he seemed to thrive during the COVID-19 pandemic while others in his industry didn't, he said he used a technique he learned in the U.S. War College called VUCA. During times of **V**olatility, **U**ncertainty, **C**omplexity, and **A**mbiguity, he learned to ask two questions:

1) What *can* I do? (Don't focus on what you can't do.)

2) What should I do *first*? (Do that right away.)[89]

Many consultants talk about the importance of "why" but miss the most important time to use it, which is in midst of change. People want to know the why behind the pivots, transitions, and transformations. When people get why you are making certain decisions, they are more likely to buy in and follow you. When leaders do not communicate the reasons behind shifts or pivots, they hinder the level of trust needed for success. In our *Trust Outlook®* study, 61% of people surveyed said that not communicating the why for change is what most hinders leaders from building trust.

Consistency in Times of Change

Bolster your resiliency during change by creating predictable patterns for communication and workflow. People need routine to be able to see where deviation is required. When companies are moving and evolving, it is critical that they maintain some level of consistency. Consider what can stay the same in times of massive change. A process? An event people look forward to? Core values? It can seem counterintuitive, but the most innovative companies often have consistency in key areas, allowing creativity and innovation to grow.

Connection in Times of Change

When people feel understood by leadership, connected to leadership, and invested in by leadership, they tend to trust leadership in the tough times.

One shining example of building trust in crisis is the Red Wing Shoe Company. They suffered a trifecta of crises in 2020 and 2021: 1) a global pandemic, 2) a supply chain crisis, and 3) a massive cyberattack. The leadership of CEO, Mark Urdahl, helped Red Wing Shoe Company weather these converging storms and become more resilient, flexible, and engaged than they have been since they first started making lifestyle footwear and leather goods in 1905.[90] How did they do it?

- They leaned into their company mission, values, and priorities. *(Clarity Pillar)*

- Urdahl and the leadership team leveraged all different types of communication in order to be transparent and candid with their workers. There was always an undertone of empathy, and a willingness to give the direct reason *why* decisions were made. *(Clarity, Compassion, and Connection Pillars)*

- They developed three guiding principles for decision-making and operations in uncharted territory. *(Character Pillar)*

    1. Ensure the safety and security of employees and their families (physical, emotional, and financial well-being).

    2. Provide business continuity (be a viable business now and into the future).

    3. Embrace our social responsibility (do what is right in the world).

- Company financials required they furlough 50% of employees, but they worked hard to make sure no furloughed employees were disadvantaged financially. With the CARES Act and a deep-seated tradition of taking care of their employees, they continued benefits for all furloughed employees and offered a pathway back to work as soon as they were able. (Compassion Pillar)

- Urdahl personally made hundreds of check-ins with employees. He held virtual and in-person meetings with customers, vendors, dealers, and employees at all levels, functions, and geographies. The effort to listen, learn, and understand the feelings around the company was a big reason Red Wing Shoes was able to thrive during this trying time. *(Connection Pillar)*

Mark Urdahl shared with me, "There was no silver bullet for garnering trust during these once-a-generation, black-swan events that were converging all at once. We had no playbook or previous experience for this. There was unifying focus of the need to rely on each other throughout the crisis. Our company's rally cry was *Together We Prevail*."

Red Wing Shoes put this slogan in local newspaper ads, community billboards, t-shirts, and coffee tumblers. More importantly, they backed up their commitment to prevail together with actions that built trust. Ultimately, every furloughed employee who wanted their job back was welcomed back.

TRUST MATTERS

CLARITY

COMPASSION

CHARACTER

COMPETENCY

COMMITMENT

CONNECTION

CONTRIBUTION

CONSISTENCY

SOLVE WITH TRUST

> *Change isn't the problem; it's how we deal with it that can be the problem!* -DH

Trust Tool #40: BUILDING TRUST THROUGH CRISIS & CHANGE™

Initiating a large-scale change effort or mitigating crisis is a serious challenge for any leader. Utilize the 8 Pillars of Trust to prepare for the next crisis...because there *will be* another crisis.

What most blocks the success of change efforts in organizations? 1) When change benefits the organization and not the individuals, and 2) when employees feel unsafe physically, emotionally, or psychologically.

Whether launching a new product, rebranding the business, or hiring new leadership, change is rarely simple. However, the greatest opportunity for leaders to develop trust is in times of change.

> **Your opportunity to build trust the fastest is during change.**

Win in Change

If trust can be maintained or even grown during challenging circumstances, leadership will be all the more trusted in times of stability. I have seen leaders win and others lose during times of change. The winners used these tactics.

Take an active approach.

People who stick their head in the sand lose. Leaders who are visibly engaged and actively managing the response to a crisis demonstrate commitment and capability, which are essential for trust. This involves not only addressing the crisis at hand but also being accessible and responsive to the concerns of those affected.

Deal with tension.

Like a violin with strings that are too loose or too tight, a leader has to constantly fine-tune the tension of seemingly true contradictions. Should I persevere through this, or should I pivot to stay alive? Should we diversify or niche? Should we take quick action or be patient? Should we start by giving the product away to grow market share, or should we charge to show value? Should I be more transparent or more confidential? Should I give grace or hold to justice on this issue?

A trusted leader needs wisdom to deal with tension well. During change, write down the obvious tensions you feel that require decisions. List pros and cons for each side of the tension (for example, persevere or pivot). Meet with trusted advisors or mentors and talk through your options to gain perspective and decide next steps. Don't make decisions alone when in crisis. This process can help you avoid major pitfalls.

Be predictable.

During a crisis, the predictability of a leader's actions becomes a calming force. Consistent leadership behaviors, such as regular updates and steady, rational decision-making, reassure stakeholders and build trust. If your people feel they're on a firm foundation with their leader, they will be more able to jump from it to something new when necessary.

Lead with compassion.

In times of crisis, people need to feel cared for first. How can you empathize and show care? A listening session? Personalized support? A message showing empathy? Creative resources? Small gestures can go a long way.

During the height of the COVID-19 pandemic, I was on a Zoom call with hundreds of exhausted nurses. I wanted to extend compassion, yet I couldn't reach each one individually. We simply didn't have time. So, to open the Zoom meeting I had them find a sheet of paper and draw a quick picture of how they were feeling. On the count of three, everyone showed the picture to the camera. I saw stick figures with tears falling to the bottom of the page. I saw big round faces that looked very angry. Without time to have all of them verbally share, this 30-second exercise made them feel seen and cared for, and it moved our conversation toward solutions more quickly. It only took a few minutes, and that bit of connection seemed to accelerate the feeling of collaboration we needed for the meeting.

Define one priority.

In times of crisis, reduce the noise and concentrate on adjusted priorities. Move resources to the essentials. You may even need to single out one top priority for a time.

I had the honor to speak with retired four-star General Stanley A. McChrystal, former commander of the United States and International Security Assistance Forces (ISAF) in Afghanistan, best known for his comprehensive counterinsurgency strategy there. At one time, General McChrystal was unable to locate a significant person of interest and so he initiated holding a dedicated daily meeting where his staff would discuss intelligence updates about the possible whereabouts of this individual. They dedicated 30 minutes for this every day, keeping it as their ONE priority, and General McChrystal and his dedicated team removed the threat in just two months! In crisis, life can be overwhelming, and change occurs quickly, but keeping your eye on the essentials will help.[91]

Seek wisdom.

The Connection Pillar is critical here. People who succeed actively reach out to mentors, friends, and counselors. If you are a leader, consider creating a personal advisory board or a Mastermind Group you can go to any time. Make sure it is made up of people who will hold you accountable, give you encouragement, and offer wisdom and resources. Don't wait for a crisis: build your support team *now*.

Think short *and* long term.

Admiral James Stockdale was the highest officer held as a prisoner of war in Hanoi during the Vietnam War: he was tortured there for more than seven years. Jim Collins, author of *Good to Great*, shared a conversation he had with the Admiral that has become known as the "Stockdale Paradox." When asked what was different about the prisoners who didn't make it out of Vietnam, Stockdale replied:

> *Oh, that's easy, the optimists. They were the ones who said, "We're going to be out by Christmas." And Christmas would come, and Christmas would go. Then they'd say, "We're going to be out by Easter." And Easter would come, and Easter would go. And then Thanksgiving, and then it would be Christmas again. And they died of a broken heart. This is a very important lesson. You must never confuse faith that you will prevail in the end—which you can never afford to lose—with the discipline to confront the most brutal facts of your current reality, whatever they might be.[92]*

Effective leaders see the short-term realities and also keep the long-term hope and vision alive.

Take care of yourself.
Prioritize keeping yourself healthy and fueled during challenging times. In crisis, check your SEEDS (Sleep, Exercise, Eating right, Drinking water, Source of strength). When leaders don't take care of themselves, everyone suffers.

Do the work.

It's Worth It

How would it change your family if all the members were trustworthy? What would your team be like if everyone pursued building the 8 Pillars of Trust? What would your organization or community look like if it were embedded in a culture of trust?

On a farm, the cows don't feed themselves, the crops don't water themselves, and the manure pile doesn't shovel itself. A garden starts as an empty plot with only a vision of what it will be. Planting, watering, cultivating, weeding, and fertilizing give the seed a chance to grow and one day bear fruit. You can't enjoy the sweet produce without doing the work first.

Like the garden, I hope you now have a vision for what a trusted culture and a trustworthy YOU could look like. You have the tools to plant, cultivate, and harvest the fruits of trust. My only guarantee is that *active, conscious, intentional work is required.* You know it's worth the time and effort.

Nothing is as fulfilling as the sense of accomplishment after healthy sacrifice and purposeful effort toward a worthy goal. Over time, you can demonstrate to yourself and others that you can be confidently believed in. You might make some mistakes, but then you will get back to the work. You will build and rebuild the Pillars of Trust. I will be doing the same. It may not be easy, but it will be worth it.

Being trustworthy takes work *every single day*. I know you can do it. Start with yourself. Pick up a Trust Tool and get to work. Be a part of making a dent in our global trust crisis.

For your life...

     for your organization...

          for those who come after us...

Trust Matters More than Ever!

Trust makes an impact

one relationship,

one family,

one company,

one country at a time!

Which Trust Tool do *you* need today?

SOLVE WITH TRUST

TOOL INDEX

CLARITY

COMPASSION

CHARACTER

COMPETENCY

COMMITMENT

CONNECTION

CONTRIBUTION

CONSISTENCY

SOLVE WITH TRUST

Acknowledgments

My best friend, cofounder, and wife, Lisa, I love you and trust you. Thank you for making me (and our work at TELI) better every day. Your energy, dedication, and deep involvement in this book drove it to completion. Vanessa, Isaiah, Maria Claire, and Micah, you have taught me a lot about why trust matters. I love being your dad. Loren, my childhood roommate and brother, you are my trusted brainstormer to this day. Ultimate thanks to God who is worthy of all my trust.

Trust Edge Leadership Institute team, your insights throughout the entire process made this book better. Heidi Sheard, my editor, and Heidi Koopman, my designer, your remarkable, on-brand, and very creative work has taken this book to the next level. Isaiah Horsager, your pillar designs were a stellar contribution to this book. They embody the strong, trusted message I've come to believe in so passionately.

BroadStreet Publishing team, especially Carlton and Michelle, thank you for this amazing partnership and for your guidance and editing work on this project. Advanced readers, your insights made this book better! Thank you, Anne, Dan, Gabe, Jerry, Jessie, Joe, Kacey, Kari, Kirby, Loren, Mikella, Nathaniel, Peggy, Sara, and Steve.

Clients and partners in this work, the inspiration and confirmation I've received from you is immeasurable! You've shown me that *Trust Matters More than Ever* and that strengthening it will bring success in both business and in life. Thanks to you, I was encouraged to bring this book to completion. YOU are the true champions of this work!

TO LEARN HOW to bring David to your event or organization, or to learn about our certification options, visit DavidHorsager.com or scan here:

DR. DAVID HORSAGER is CEO of Trust Edge Leadership Institute, inventor of the Enterprise Trust Index™, and director of the global research publication, the *Trust Outlook*®. Horsager is a *Wall Street Journal* bestselling author and senior fellow at Indiana Wesleyan University. His decades of trust work have served as a catalyst for trust awareness and development across the globe.

Horsager has advised leaders and taught the Trust Edge framework to organizations ranging from Delta Airlines, McDonald's, FedEx, and Toyota to the New York Yankees, Walmart, Zoom, MIT, and global governments.

Horsager was inducted into the National Speakers Association's Speaker Hall of Fame (CSP, CPAE) in 2017. His board work with a wide variety of industries continues to inspire his research, consulting, and writing. The mission of Horsager and his team at Trust Edge Leadership Institute is to develop trusted leaders and organizations.

The youngest of six siblings, Horsager learned many of his life lessons growing up on a farm in northern Minnesota. A belief in the goodness of humanity and endless possibilities has propelled him throughout his career. David and his wife, Lisa, started this work in 1999, and Lisa continues to serve as culture ambassador at the institute. The Horsagers have four children and live on a hobby farm where they enjoy the outdoors and host lively discussions around the campfire.

Endnotes

The *Trust Oulook*® references come from an annual global research study conducted by Trust Edge Leadership Institute. You can find those publications archived here: TrustEdge.com/the-research/

1   Marno, Hanna, "Infants prefer a Trustworthy Person: An Early Sign of Social Cognition in Infants," National Institute of Health: National Library of Medicine, ncbi.nlm.nih.gov, May 20, 2024.

2   Krauss Whitbourne, Susan, "There May Be More to First Impressions Than You Realize," psychologytoday.com, June 29, 2021.

3   "The Four Factors of Trust: How Organizations Can Earn Lifelong Loyalty, Deloitte, deloitte.com, November 1, 2022.

4   Ratanjee, Vibhas, "How to Build Trust in the Workplace," gallup.com, September 2023.

5   Gura, David, "It Cost $22 Billion to Rescue Two Failed Banks. Now the Question Is Who Will Pay," npr.org, April 2023.

6   "The Catholic Church Has Paid Nearly $4 Billion Over Sexual Abuse Claims, Group Says," newsweek.com, August 2018.

7   Rovell, Darren, "Estimated Deflategate Cost: $22.5 Million," espn.com, June 2016.

8   "Volkswagen Says Diesel Scandal Has Cost it 31.3 Billion Euros," reuters.com, March 2020.

9   Zak, Paul J., "The Neuroscience of Trust," hbr.org, February 2017.

10 *Public Trust in Government: 1958-2023*, Pew Research Center's Forum on Trust in Government, pewresearch.org, September 19, 2023.

11 Jamison, Peter, et al, "Home Schooling's Rise From Fringe to Fastest-Growing Form of Education," washingtonpost.com, October 31, 2023.

12 Jones, Jeffrey, "U.S. Church Attendance Still Lower Than Pre-Pandemic," news.gallup.com, June 26, 2023.

13 Leslie, Jack, "The Crisis of Trust in Public Health," thinkglobalhealth.org, February 14, 2023.

14 "From Businesses and Banks to Colleges and Churches: Americans' Views of U.S. Institutions," pewresearch.org, March 26, 2024.

15 Maese, Ellyn, "Almost a Quarter of the World Feels Lonely," gallup.com, October 24, 2023.

16 "Our Epidemic of Loneliness and Isolation," hhs.gov, March 25, 2024.

17 "Dissociative Disorders," MayoClinic.com, mayoclinic.org, March 6, 2024.

18 Cox, Daniel A., "The (Political) News Is Too Negative," americansurveycenter.org, November 2, 2023.

19 Arend, Richard J., "The Costs of Ambiguity in Strategic Contexts," mdpi.com, August 2022.

20 "Conflict in the Workplace Statistics," gitnux.org, December 2023.

21 Gambill, Tony, "5 Characteristics of High-Trust Teams," forbes.com, July 2022.

22 Clear, James, "How Long Does it Actually Take to Form a New Habit? (Backed by Science)," jamesclear.com, May 3, 2024.

23 Christian Espinosa, christianespinosa.com, March 2, 2024.

24 Ernst & Young, LLP, "2023 EY Empathy in Business Survey," ey.com, March 2023.

25 "Top 10 Airlines Ranked Best to Worst," gizmodo.com, April 23, 2024.

26 Thorson, Angela, "Helping People, Changing Lives: 3 Health Benefits of Volunteering," mayoclinichealthsystem.org, August 1, 2023.

27 "2023 Work in America Survey," www.apa.org, March 4, 2024.

28 SIY Global, "The Three Pillars of Leading with Compassion," siyglobal.com, May 30, 2024.

29 "Feeling gratitude and not expressing it is like wrapping a present and not giving it," brainyquote.com, March 17, 2024.

30 Maya Angelou Quotes, goodreads.com, February 29, 2024.

31 Mejja, Zameena, "3 Ways to Get People to Trust You, According to a Havard Expert Who Trained Uber Execs," cnbc.com, May 18, 2018.

32 "Conflict at Work: A Research Report", themyersbriggs.com, August 2022.

33 Brower, Tracy, "Why Workplaces Shouldn't Try to Be Fun," fastcompany.com, April 6, 2023.

34 "Character in the Workplace Has Powerfully Positive Ripple Effects," your.yale.edu, April 29, 2024.

35 "Bentley-Gallup Business in Society Report," gallup.com, 2023.

36 "The 2011 State of the Industry: Increased Commitment to Workplace Learning," researchgate.net, November 2011.

37 Office of Public Affairs: U.S. Department of Justice, "Wells Fargo Bank Agrees to Pay $1.2 Billion for Improper Mortgage Lending Practices", www.justice.gov, April 2016.

38 U.S. Department of Justice, "Wells Fargo Agrees to Pay $3 Billion to Resolve Criminal and Civil Investigations into Sales Practices Involving the Opening of Millions of Accounts without Customer Authorization," justice.gov, February 2020.

39 "Story of the Four-Way Test by Herbert J. Taylor," rotary5630.org, April 15, 2024.

40 "Guiding Principles," my.rotary.org, April 15, 2024.

41 "Rudolf Clausius," britannica.com, February 2024.

42 "Leading Quick Service Restaurant Chains in the United States in 2022," statista.com, August 2023. This is a graphical representation of the data. You can also read the full report by searching for "The 2023 QSR 50: Fast Food's Leading Annual Report."

43 "The 2022 QSR® Drive-Thru Report, qsrmagazine.com, March 16, 2024.

44 "Lessons Learned from Chick-fil-A's Team Management Approach," blog. belaysolutions.com, May 30, 2024.

45 Cantrell, Griffiths, Jones, and Hiipakka, "Building Tomorrow's Skills-Based Organization," deloitte.com, March 7, 2024.

46 "Future of jobs 2023: These are the most in-demand skills now – and beyond," weforum.org, May 1, 2023.

47 Day, Roanna, "The More Children Read, the More They End Up Earning," redonline.co.uk, April 26, 2018.

48 "Time Spent Reading," amacad.org, May 21, 2024.

49 "mentor," merriam-webster.com, March 7, 2024.

50 Ericsson, Anders, et all, "The Making of an Expert," hbr.org, April 18, 2024.

51 Peck, Sarah Kathleen, "Why Your Most Important Business Move Might Be Joining a Mastermind," forbes.com, February 2018.

52 Piper, Watty, *The Little Engine That Could*, (New York City: Grosset & Dunlap, 2001).

53 Pendell, Ryan, "Employee Engagement Strategies: Fixing the World's $8.8 Trillion Problem," gallup.com, June 2022.

54 Clear, James, *Atomic Habits: An Easy & Proven Way to Build Good Habits & Break Bad Ones*, (New York City: Avery, 2018).

55 "Are You Accountable?" becomingyourbest.com, March 26, 2024.

56 "Employee Loyalty Is Declining. Here's How to Build it Back," weforum. org, November 2021.

57 Stulberg, Brad, "The Perils of Heroic Individualism," bstulberg.medium. com, September 18, 2022.

58 "Rwandan Genocide," history.com, May 19, 2023.

59 De Dieu Kayiranga, Jean, "Sustainable peace for sustainable development – A global challenge that calls for collective action," undp.org, November 2023.

60 Africa: Safety Index by Country 2024, numbeo.com, April 2024. See also, "Rwanda the 6th safest country for solo travellers, new survey finds," euronews.com, April 2024.

61 This also came from my conversations with Dr. Antoine Rutayisire, a leader in the Rwandan Reconciliation efforts. For further reading, I highly recommend his book, *Reconciliation is My Lifestyle: A Life's Lesson on Forgiving and Loving Those Who Have Hated You*.

62 "The History of the Lightbulb," energy.gov, November 22, 2013.

63 "Cotton Gin and Eli Whitney," history.com, February 4, 2010.

64 Umberson, D., & Karas Montez, J. "Social Relationships and Health: A Flashpoint for Health Policy," Journal of Health and Social Behavior, 51(1_ suppl), S54-S66, doi.org, October 8, 2010.

65 TED Talk, Susan Pinker, "The Secret to Living Longer May Be Your Social Life," www.ted.com, April 2017.

66 Ludmir, Clara, "How Lululemon, Starbucks, and Google Boost Brand Engagement Through Community Retail," forbes.com, May 24, 2023.

67 Laoyan, Sarah, "Organizational Silos: 4 Common Issues and How to Prevent Them," asana.com, January 2024.

68 Patel, Alok and Plowman, Stephanie, "The Increasing Importance of a Best Friend at Work," gallup.com, 2022.

69 Wooll, Maggie, "Your Workforce is Lonely. It's Hurting Your Business." The Connection Crisis, betterup.com, June 2022.

70 Harney, Sarah, "Putnam's Paradox," governing.com, August 2010.

71 "Leading with Culture Intelligence," davidlivermore.com, May 2, 2024.

72 "Health Benefits of Gratitude," uclahealth.org, March 22, 2023.

73 "Iodice, Malouff, and Schutte, "The Association Between Gratitude and Depression: A Meta-Analysis," ClinMedJournals.org, March 17, 2024.

74 Brockington, Guilherme, et al, "Storytelling Increases Oxytocin and Positive Emotions and Decreases Cortisol and Pain in Hospitalized Children," Proceedings of the National Academy of Sciences, doi.org, May 24, 2021.

75 Choy, Esther, "Storytelling Is a Must-Have Leadership Skill for the 21st Century," forbes.com, September 10, 2023.

76 "Lessons Learned from Walmart's Don Soderquist," workmatters.org, August 2, 2016.

77 Schwantes, Marcel, "Warren Buffett Says This Is the Single Greatest Skill to Boost Your Career and Improve Your Worth," inc.com, March 13, 2024.

78 Gallo, Carmine, *Talk Like Ted: The 9 Public Speaking Secrets of the World's Top Minds*, (Hodder and Stoughton: London), 2019.

79 Dhingra, Naina, et al, "Help Your Employees Find Purpose – or Watch Them Leave," mckinsey.com, April 5, 2021.

80 "The Value of Belongs at Work: New Frontiers for Inclusion in 2021 and Beyond," betterup.com, 2019.

81 "Small Business Statistics 2022 Recap: What Is the Small Business Failure/Success Rate," linkedin, March 31, 2023.

82 Abadi, Mark, "A CEO and dad uses a 100-year-old strategy to get control of his schedule in just 15 minutes each night," businessinsider.com, September 2018.

83 Jamal, Natasha and Dvorak, Nate, "Consistent Cultures Deliver Customer Value," gallup.com, March 2020.

84 "Repeaters," tutorialspoint.com, March 4, 2024.

85 Taylor, Kory, Jones, Elizabeth B., "Adult Dehydration," ncbi.nlm.nih.gov, October 3, 2022.

86 Mark 12:30-31 New International Version, *Holy Bible*, bible.com, March 8, 2024. This is also widely known in many cultures as "the Golden Rule."

87 Ruppert, Dr. Steven, "The Main Cultural Differences Between China & Germany Pt 2 – Task-Orientation vs Relationship-Orientation," linkedin.com, September 30, 2020.

88 "Presidential Approval Ratings – George W. Bush," news.gallup.com, May 21, 2024.

89 Kan, Paul, Whitt, Jacqueline E., Hill, Andrew A., "Is 'VUCA' a Useful Term or Is it All 'VUCA'ED' Up?", warroom.armywarcollege.edu, July 13, 2018.

90 "Red Wing Shoes Our Story," redwingshoes.com, May 21, 2024.

91 If you are intrigued by the story of General Stan McChrystal, you can read more about him on his website: mcchrystalgroup.com.

92 Groysberg, Boris and Abrahams, Robin, "What the Stockdale Paradox Tells Us About Crisis Leadership," hbswk.hbs.edu, May 10, 2024.

HORSAGER
LEADERSHIP

HORSAGER LEADERSHIP PRESS is part of the Horsager Leadership Inc. family of companies, including Trust Edge Leadership Institute (www.trustedge.com). Based in Saint Paul, Minnesota, our mission is to develop trusted leaders and organizations around the world. Since 1999, we have pioneered leadership development through research, speaking, publications, human capital development, and consulting, all based on the importance of trust and its proven impact around the world.

Our books aim to inspire and equip leaders and organizations with a high level of trustworthiness. For research, resources, and tools, visit www.HorsagerLeadership.com or call 651-340-6555.